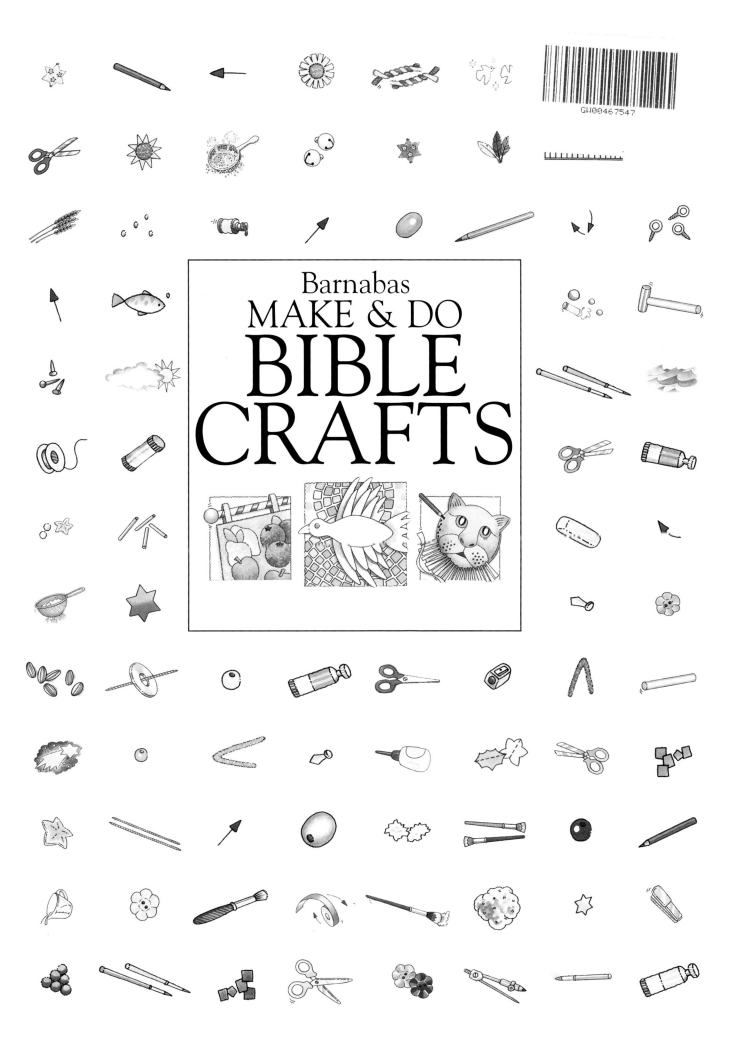

Barnabas
MAKE & DO
BIBLE
CRAFTS

Published by The Bible Reading Fellowship
15 The Chambers, Vineyard
Abingdon, OX14 3FE
United Kingdom
Tel: +44 (0)1865 319700
Email: enquiries@brf.org.uk
Website: www.brf.org.uk

ISBN 978 1 84101 642 9

First edition 2005
This edition 2008

Editorial Director Annette Reynolds
Project Editor Leena Lane
Art Director Gerald Rogers
Pre-production Krystyna Hewitt
Production John Laister

British Library Cataloguing in Publication Data.
A catalogue record for this book is available from
the British Library.

Printed and bound in Singapore

Barnabas
MAKE & DO
BIBLE
CRAFTS

Imaginative craft ideas
that bring the stories of the Bible to life

GILLIAN CHAPMAN AND LEENA LANE

CONTENTS

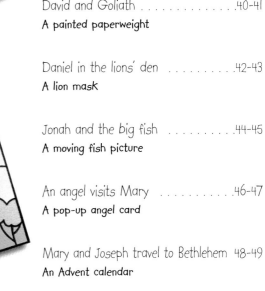

CONTENTS

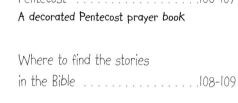

8

HOW TO USE THIS BOOK

You will find within this book a wealth of ideas and inspiration for using with children, at home or in the classroom.

Discover fresh ideas for bringing Old and New Testament stories to life and for celebrating Christmas and Easter.

Craft ideas vary from the very simple to the more challenging, but the emphasis is strongly on using inexpensive materials and equipment, using recycled and domestic materials where possible. Children will experience the thrill of making something wonderful almost 'out of nothing'.

To help keep preparation time to a minimum, each project spread features:

✳ a lively retelling of the Bible story, suitable for reading aloud to a group

✳ a list of materials needed

✳ clear step-by-step instructions

✳ a photograph of how the finished article may look, in case you haven't had time to make one earlier!

All the craft ideas have been designed, tried and tested by Gillian Chapman, a well-known author of craft books. Drawing on her experience of running children's workshops on making books, masks and other crafts, she has prepared a helpful section of Bible craft tips and safety recommendations.

It is worth taking a few moments to read through this section before you begin.

Part of the excitement and satisfaction of 'Make & Do' crafts begins when children are able to develop their own original slant on an idea or design, whatever the results! Some children (and adults, let's face it) may struggle to follow instructions and lose interest very quickly if they feel an activity is too difficult. Bearing that in mind, most of the ideas in this book can be modified according to a child's ability. For example, where sewing is involved, you may use PVA glue instead; where drawing is involved, you may cut pictures out of magazines.

Specific projects, such as masks or helmets, could be used as props for drama productions. Having read the story and made the articles, children can enjoy the further dimension of bringing a story to life themselves through drama or dance.

There are several ideas for making gifts, for example, the Christmas gift bags and the Pentecost prayer book. Other craft activities will produce beautiful decorations for your classroom, church or home, such as the star mobile and the lampstand picture.

There are endless possibilities for using 'Barnabas Make & Do Bible Crafts' to explore the Bible. Enjoy them!

BIBLE CRAFT TIPS
Additional practical information

Safety First

All tools and equipment must be used with care and respect! Sharp pencils, scissors and needles can all be dangerous if used incorrectly.

However, an adult will need to help with carpentry tools and cutting tools.

If you need to use a craft knife make sure you also use a cutting board.

Shaped scissors

Special scissors with a shaped cutting blade are increasingly available for craftwork. Use these, or pinking shears, to give paper and fabric a special patterned edge.

Paints

Poster paints are great for painting on paper and card, and to paint models made from paper pulp and papier mâché. They also come in metallic colours. Acrylic paints are better for painting wooden surfaces.

A jar of clean water will be needed to mix paints and to clean brushes. Change the water frequently to keep colours looking bright. Paints can be mixed on a palette or an old plate.

For detailed drawing of animals, figures and faces sketch in the outlines first with pencil, then colour in using coloured pencils. If you have a set of watercolour paints and a fine brush, use these.

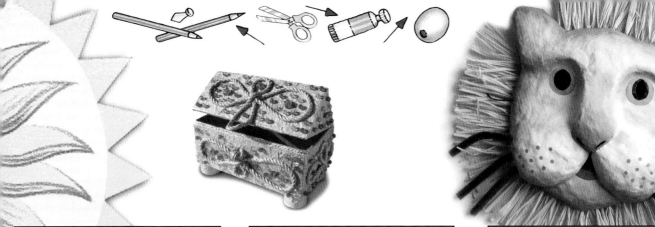

Glues

PVA glue is perfect for most craftwork. It can be diluted for papier mâché type projects. It will stick paper, card and most fabrics – but in most cases it must be used very sparingly. It will wash off with cold water.

Glue sticks are better for neat finishes, but only work on paper and thin card.

When using PVA to do fine work, such as gluing beads and sequins on to fabric, try to buy the glue in a bottle with a fine nozzle. If you don't have such a container, then pour some of the glue into a small plastic container (such as a lid) and use a cocktail stick to put tiny blobs of glue where it is needed.

Brushes

Keep separate brushes for painting and gluing. Always clean them in warm soapy water after use and dry them before putting them away.

Keeping Clean

Make sure all work surfaces are protected with newspaper and all clothing is covered with overalls (e.g. an old shirt) or an apron. Keep an old towel handy for drying not-so-clean hands.

GOD MADE THE WORLD

The story of creation

God made the light and the darkness.

God made big, tall mountains, and deep blue seas.

God made plants and flowers and trees and filled the land with them.

God made the round, spinning earth, the red hot sun and the silvery moon. He made twinkling stars and planets.

God filled the sea with slippery, shiny fish and the air with birds that chatter and sing.

God filled the land with animals of every kind, tall and short, prickly and furry, striped and spotted and patterned.

'Now I will make people,' said God. God made a man and a woman who could think and feel and love, and be his friends. He made a beautiful garden for them to live in called the Garden of Eden.

God was pleased with everything he had made. It was very good.

Make this wall frieze to illustrate the creation story.

You will need:

✂

7 sheets of card

White paper

Pencil

Coloured pencils or paints and paint brush

Scissors

Pair of compasses

Sticky tape

Split pin

Glue stick

Ruler

Magazine pictures of birds, fish, animals and people

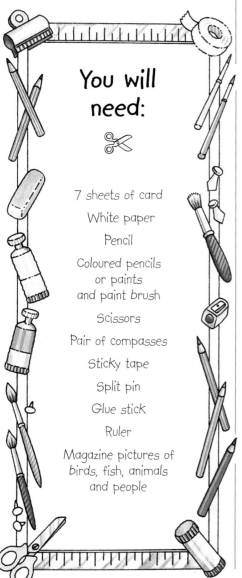

1 Draw a curve across the top of a piece of card and cut out. Use this first card as a template to draw the curve on to the remaining cards. When the curves are cut out, all the cards will be the same shape.

2 Place two cards side by side leaving a small space between them. Tape the cards together with lengths of sticky tape. Join all the cards together in the same way, taping along the front and back of each card to make a strong hinge.

3 Draw pictures to illustrate the first, second and third days of creation on sheets of white paper. Colour in with paints or coloured pencils. Cut around the drawings so they fit neatly on to the frieze panels and glue in place.

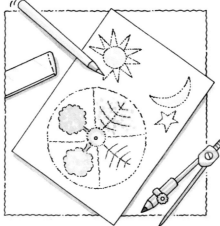

4 Try making a Seasons Wheel for the fourth day of creation. Use the compasses to draw a circle on the white paper and divide it into four. In each quarter draw a tree at different seasons of the year. Decorate the rest of the page and glue to the frieze.

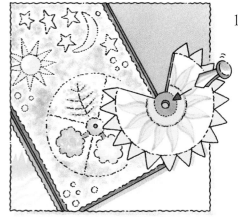

5 Draw a circle on white paper and divide into four. Draw a zig-zag pattern around the circle to make a sun shape. Colour in and cut out, leaving a quarter of the sun cut out. Attach the sun to the centre of the tree circle with a split pin.

6 Draw pictures to illustrate the fifth, sixth and seventh days of creation. You could cut out animal pictures from magazines and stick them to your drawings. Carefully cut around the finished drawings and glue them to the correct frieze panels.

Create your own frieze to whatever size and design you like.

NOAH'S ARK

The floating zoo

Noah was a good man, but all around him there was trouble.

God had made a wonderful world, but the people had spoilt everything.

There was fighting everywhere.

God told Noah what he planned to do. He was going to send a great flood.

God told Noah to build a boat and to fill it with two of every kind of animal on the earth.

God would keep them safe in the boat when the flood came.

Noah built a huge wooden boat called an ark. They covered it with tar to keep out the water. It would float on the waters until the flood was over.

Noah packed food for his family and all the animals.

They were ready for the day when the rain began and the rivers burst into flood.

God promised to keep them safe.

Make an ark and animal cards to help remember the story of Noah.

You will need:

Sheet of A3 thin coloured card

Sheets of A4 thin coloured card

Scissors

Pencil

Glue stick

Scraps of coloured paper for decoration

1 To make the folder, fold the sheet of A3 card in half, press firmly along the crease and open up. Take a sheet of A4 card, fold in half lengthways, open up and cut along the fold. Cut the top corners off these two strips.

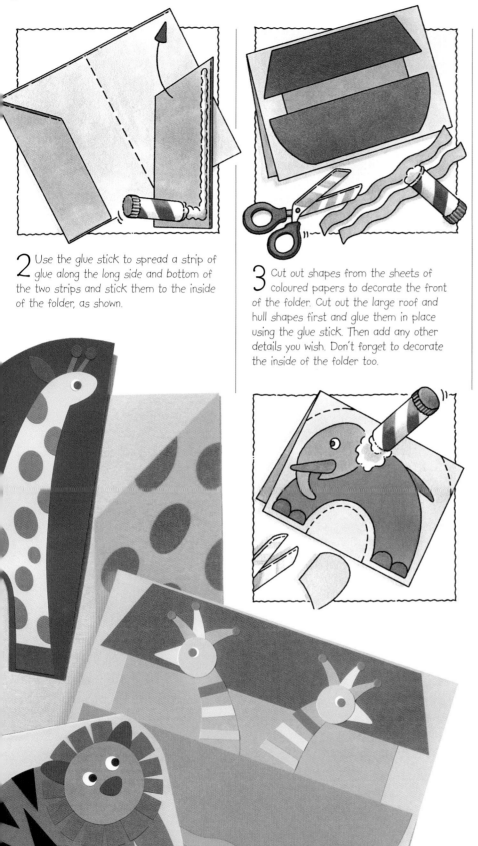

15

2 Use the glue stick to spread a strip of glue along the long side and bottom of the two strips and stick them to the inside of the folder, as shown.

3 Cut out shapes from the sheets of coloured papers to decorate the front of the folder. Cut out the large roof and hull shapes first and glue them in place using the glue stick. Then add any other details you wish. Don't forget to decorate the inside of the folder too.

4 To make the cards, cut a sheet of A4 card in half, then fold each piece in half. Decorate the cards with simple animal shapes cut out from the coloured papers. Start by drawing and cutting out body shapes, then heads. Place the pieces on the card first before sticking down to make sure they are the right size and check that the card folds are at the top.

5 Try to make the animals as colourful as possible. Cut out features, like ears, tails, tusks, spots and stripes and use the glue stick to glue them neatly into place. When all the pieces are stuck down, shape the top corners of the card and cut out the space between the legs, cutting through both sides of the card.

6 The tall giraffe card is made in the same way, but the fold of the card runs along the left side. Try making lots of different shaped cards. Small gift tags are made from a single thickness of card, threaded with string. Keep all your animal cards in the ark folder, so they are handy for that unexpected birthday!

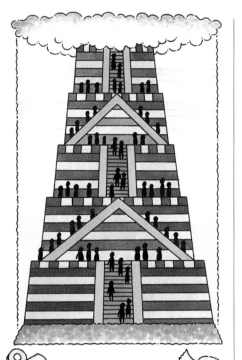

THE TOWER OF BABEL

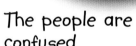

You will need:

Cardboard tubes
of different sizes
with plastic lids
e.g. empty biscuit
and crisp tubes

Glue stick

Scraps of
coloured papers

Sticky tape

Sheet of wrapping paper

Scissors

Coloured felt tipped pens

Coloured stickers or stamps
(if you have them)
for added decoration

Words, messages
and phrases in as many
different languages
as you can find

The people are confused

At first, all the people in the world spoke the same language. They moved about from place to place, looking for somewhere to settle.

'Let's make our own city with bricks,' they said. So they baked bricks in the hot sun.

When they had enough bricks, they took some tar to stick them together. They started to build their city.

'Let's build a tower that reaches to the sky!' they said. 'Then everyone will know how clever and important we are.'

But God saw what they were planning. He knew they were forgetting about the way he wanted them to live. So God mixed up their language. They couldn't understand each other any more! It all sounded like babble. God scattered the people all over the earth. Now they didn't seem as clever or as important as God.

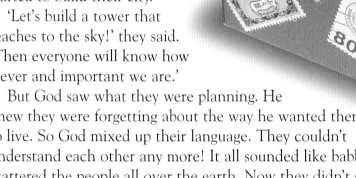

When you are copying words or characters in a language that is unfamiliar to you be very careful, as a small slip of the pen may give the word the wrong meaning or make it completely meaningless!

Make these tower boxes and decorate them with foreign stamps or writing.

TOWER PENCIL CASE

1 Make sure the cardboard tube is clean inside before you begin and tall enough to hold all your pencils! Then cover it with wrapping paper. Lay the tube on the paper to measure the correct width and trim the paper to size.

2 Spread a thin layer of glue on to the paper using the glue stick and carefully wrap the paper around the tube. Secure the join of the paper with a length of sticky tape.

3 Write out words and phrases in different languages on small scraps of coloured paper. Either copy these from books or if you have friends that speak a different language, ask them to write out messages for you to copy.

4 Glue these paper messages on to the tube along with small paper shapes or coloured stickers or stamps to decorate the tubes. Don't forget to decorate the lid.

TOWER DESK TIDY

5 This is made in exactly the same way as the pencil case, but you don't need such a tall tube or a lid. Choose a container that will hold all your writing equipment so you can see exactly where it is when you need it!

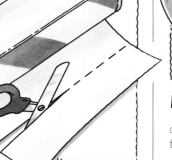

18

GOD'S PROMISE TO ABRAHAM

A baby son for Abraham and Sarah

Abram was a good man who followed God. He left his home to settle in a new land which God showed him.

God promised to make Abram's family very important for many years to come. The problem was, Abram and his wife Sarai could not have children. Without children, their family could not grow any bigger.

But one day God told Abram that he would have a son and a very large family.

'Look at the stars and try to count them,' said God. 'You will have as many people in your family as the number of stars you can see.'

Imagine how amazed Abram felt about that!

Abram was now an old man and had thought he would never have any children. But he trusted God and believed his special promise.

When Abram was ninety-nine years old, God's promise started to come true!

God gave Abram a new name – Abraham. And… a new son! Abraham named his son Isaac, which means 'laughter'.

You will need:

✂

Thin card

Pair of compasses

Ruler and pencil

Scissors

Pieces of felt

Embroidery cotton and needle

PVA glue

Felt tipped pen

Assorted beads and sequins

Cotton wool

Make this star mobile to help you remember God's promise to Abraham.

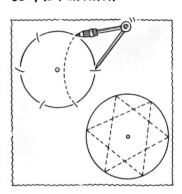

1 First, you will need to make some star templates. Use the compasses to draw a 15cm diameter circle on the card. Keeping the position of the compass points the same, use them to mark six points around the circumference of the circle. Join up these points to make a star.

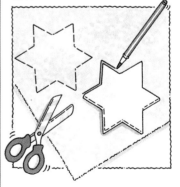

2 Make two more star shapes from 10cm and 5cm diameter circles and cut them out. Use the card templates to make the felt stars. Place the template on the felt, draw around it with a felt tipped pen and cut it out with scissors. You will need 2 x 15cm stars, 6 x 10cm stars and 6 x 5cm stars.

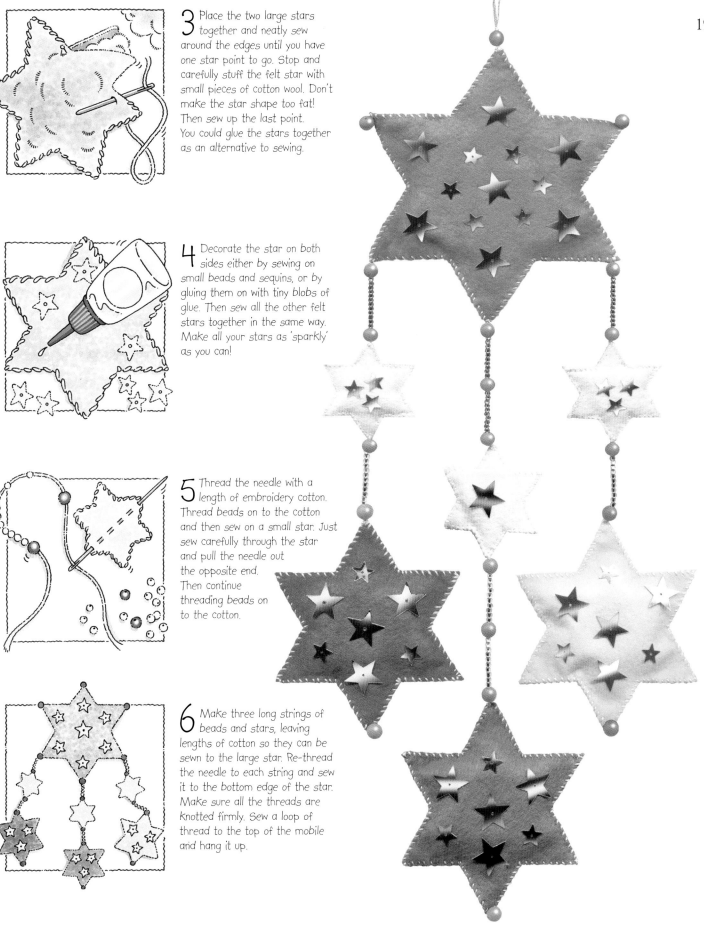

3 Place the two large stars together and neatly sew around the edges until you have one star point to go. Stop and carefully stuff the felt star with small pieces of cotton wool. Don't make the star shape too fat! Then sew up the last point. You could glue the stars together as an alternative to sewing.

4 Decorate the star on both sides either by sewing on small beads and sequins, or by gluing them on with tiny blobs of glue. Then sew all the other felt stars together in the same way. Make all your stars as 'sparkly' as you can!

5 Thread the needle with a length of embroidery cotton. Thread beads on to the cotton and then sew on a small star. Just sew carefully through the star and pull the needle out the opposite end. Then continue threading beads on to the cotton.

6 Make three long strings of beads and stars, leaving lengths of cotton so they can be sewn to the large star. Re-thread the needle to each string and sew it to the bottom edge of the star. Make sure all the threads are knotted firmly. Sew a loop of thread to the top of the mobile and hang it up.

You will need:

Piece of white card

Scissors

Pencil

Ruler

Length of thick coloured fabric or felt

PVA glue and brush

Scraps of multicoloured fabrics

Trimmings and buttons for decoration

Length of braid

6 brass curtain rings

Needle and thread

REBEKAH'S KINDNESS

A surprise meeting at the well

Make this colourful frieze and think of Rebekah watering all those camels!

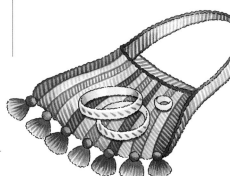

Every evening Rebekah fetched water from the well for her family.

One day, she noticed a man standing at the well with his ten camels.

'Please give me a drink,' he said.

Rebekah offered him some water and then gave the camels a drink too. They had travelled a long way and were very thirsty.

Then Rebekah had a surprise! The man took a beautiful gold ring and gold bracelets out of his bag and put them on Rebekah. She had never seen anything so fine!

'Take me to your father's house,' he said. So they set off to see Rebekah's family.

There was another surprise later that day. The man said that God had guided him to find a wife for his master's son. His master was Abraham; Isaac was his son. He asked if Rebekah would go with him and become Isaac's wife. She agreed and set off the next day to marry Isaac.

1 Draw a simple outline of a camel on the white card and cut it out carefully. Use this shape as a template to make all the fabric camels.

2 Lay the template on a piece of fabric, draw around the shape and cut out the fabric camel. Repeat this until you have ten camels cut from different fabrics.

3 Make the frieze background from a strip of fabric long enough to take a row of ten camels. To make a rough calculation of the length, measure the width of one camel and multiply it by ten.

4 Glue the camels to the background frieze with small blobs of PVA glue. Start at the left side of the frieze and overlap the camels so that the tail overlaps the neck of the previous one.

5 When all the camels are glued in place, decorate the frieze with small buttons, beads or any trimmings you have. Glue a length of braid to the top and bottom edges.

6 Sew the curtain rings at intervals along the top edge of the frieze. These represent the jewellery given to Rebekah at the well and can be used to hang up the frieze.

JACOB AND ESAU
A tasty stew

Esau and Jacob were twin brothers, sons of Isaac and Rebekah.

Esau had red hair and was very hairy. He was a skilful hunter and loved being outdoors.

Jacob was a quiet man who liked staying at home. He loved cooking.

Esau was born first, which meant that when his father died, Esau would be given all that his father owned and a special blessing. Jacob secretly wanted to be the one to get this, so he planned to trick his brother.

One day, when Esau came home from hunting, he was very hungry. He could smell a delicious stew that Jacob had been cooking.

'Give me some of that stew,' he asked Jacob.

'Only if you promise to let me be the one who gets Dad's special blessing,' said Jacob.

Esau couldn't resist the stew any longer, so he promised to let Jacob have their father's blessing and all he owned. Esau only cared about his hungry tummy!

Jacob was very pleased that his trick had worked.

You will need:

✂

Sketching paper and pencil

Felt tipped pen

Sheet of sandpaper and thick card

Scissors

PVA glue

Glue spreader or brush

Collage materials: dried aduki and haricot beans, lentils, green split peas, pasta shapes and sunflower seeds*

* Please remind children that raw beans are not edible and small peas could be a choking hazard.

1 Sketch out your design on paper. Draw the stewpot and the ladle. Decorate the pot with patterns and have some steam rising out of the top. Finally draw a patterned border around your design.

2 Use the PVA to glue the sandpaper to a sheet of thick card and leave to dry. The sandpaper will give the collage a lovely textured background. Trim the sandpaper to the same size as your design.

Make this collage stewpot and think about Jacob's trick.

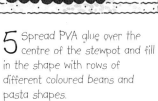

5 Spread PVA glue over the centre of the stewpot and fill in the shape with rows of different coloured beans and pasta shapes.

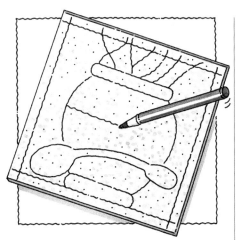

3 Following the design, sketch the outlines of the main shapes on to the sandpaper using a felt tipped pen. This will give you guidelines when you start assembling the collage.

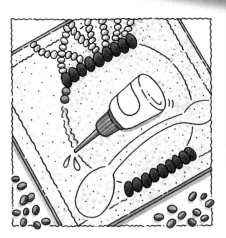

4 Begin with the main shapes. Spread the glue along the outlines and press the beans into the glue. Work around the stewpot, the lines of steam and fill in the ladle.

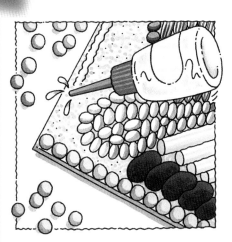

6 Spread the glue along the lines of the border pattern and press a row of beans around the edge. The PVA glue will dry clear so there shouldn't be any blobs of glue showing when it dries.

JOSEPH'S COAT

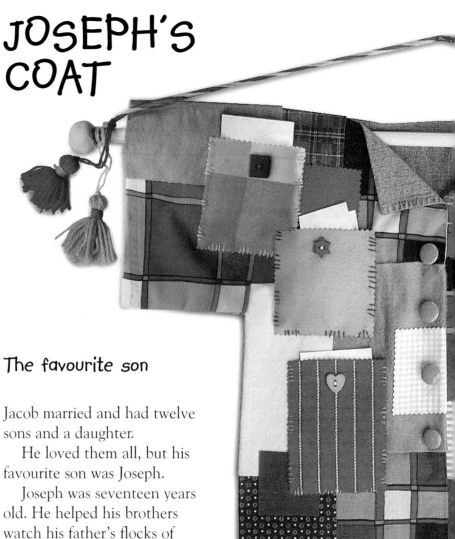

You will need:

✂

Large piece of scrap fabric for patchwork lining

Felt tipped pen

Smaller scraps of multicoloured fabrics

Scissors

Sewing needle, thread and pins

PVA glue and brush

Darning needle and coloured yarns

Extra trimmings, buttons and beads for decoration

Special messages written on pieces of paper

Length of dowel (and some adult help)

2 balls of plasticine

The favourite son

Jacob married and had twelve sons and a daughter.

He loved them all, but his favourite son was Joseph.

Joseph was seventeen years old. He helped his brothers watch his father's flocks of sheep.

As a special present, Jacob gave Joseph a wonderful coat to wear.

Joseph was very pleased, but his brothers were jealous.

Why did their father love him more than he loved them?

Why couldn't they all have a splendid coat?

The coat made the brothers jealous.

They didn't want Joseph to be more important than they were.

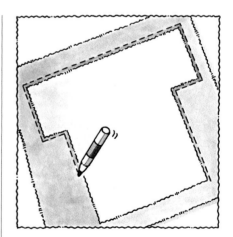

Use a felt tipped pen to draw a large 'T' shape on to the fabric and cut it out. Then use the shape as a template to cut out a second identical shape. These shapes will form the lining of the patchwork hanging, so their size and shape will determine the size of the finished hanging.

Make this patchwork hanging to help you remember the special coat Joseph wore.

2 Lay the two shapes on top of each other and pin together. Cut the top shape in half, along the centre and around the collar. Use the sewing needle and thread to sew the shapes together across the shoulders and along the sides as shown, or glue them together if preferred.

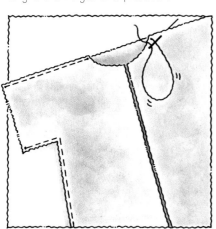

3 Cut out lots of square patches from your collection of fabric scraps. They can be all different sizes. Begin to glue the patches to the lining. Start at the bottom and use the glue very sparingly!

4 Work up both sides of the coat, keeping the two halves separate. Overlap the patches so the lining fabric is completely covered. If you have enough patches, also cover the back of the coat.

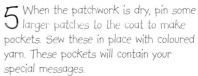

5 When the patchwork is dry, pin some larger patches to the coat to make pockets. Sew these in place with coloured yarn. These pockets will contain your special messages.

6 Use any trimmings and buttons to make the patchwork coat as colourful as possible. To make a hanger, thread the dowel through the coat so 3cm show from each sleeve and ask an adult to cut the dowel to size. Place a ball of plasticine on each end. Tie coloured yarns around the dowel to hang up the coat.

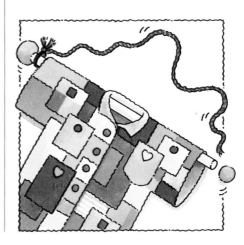

JOSEPH'S DREAMS
The jealous brothers

Joseph's brothers didn't like him very much. Not only was he their father's favourite, Joseph started telling them stories about odd dreams he had been having.

'Listen!' said Joseph. 'We were all in the field tying up the wheat into sheaves. Suddenly my sheaf got up and yours stood round it in a circle. Then your sheaves all bowed down to mine!'

The brothers didn't like the sound of that at all! Or what came next…

'Hey! I've had another dream!' said Joseph. The brothers groaned.

'I dreamed I saw the sun, moon and eleven stars all bowing down to me!'

Joseph's eleven brothers didn't like it at all. They started to plan how to get rid of him, and found a way to sell him to some traders – as a slave in Egypt.

You will need:

Small notebook with a plain cover

Scissors

Wrapping paper and textured papers

Glue stick

Dried grasses or stems of wheat

PVA glue and brush

Sheets of A4 thin card to make cards and bookmarks (optional)

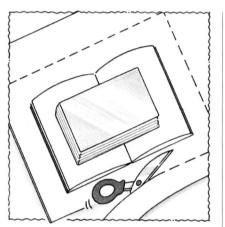

1 Spread the open notebook on top of the sheet of wrapping paper with the reverse side of the paper facing upwards. Hold the notebook in place by placing a heavier book on top of it. Trim off any excess paper to approximately 3cm (or a ruler's width) all round.

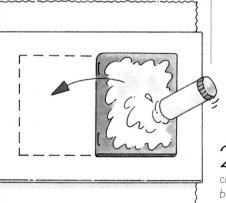

2 Close the notebook, keeping it in place on the paper. Spread glue over the front cover using the glue stick. Then open the book so that the paper sticks to the cover.

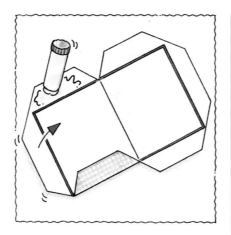

3 Close the notebook again from the back and cover the back cover and the spine with glue. Open the notebook so that the paper sticks to the back cover.

4 Trim away the corners of the paper as shown here, and the excess paper at the spine. Crease these paper flaps and glue them to the inside of the covers. Smooth all over the new paper cover with your hands, making sure it has stuck firmly.

5 Take a piece of textured paper slightly smaller than the notebook cover and cut two small slots across the centre as shown. Glue around the edge of the paper and stick it to the front cover, leaving the slots unglued.

Decorate a notebook with wheat or dried grasses to remind you of Joseph's dreams.

6 Thread dried grasses or stems of wheat through the slots and glue them in place with small blobs of PVA glue. Look at the ideas photographed here and use this same method to decorate greetings cards and bookmarks.

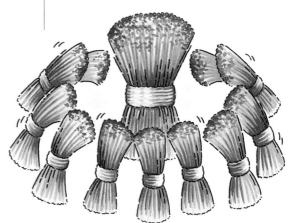

JOSEPH INTERPRETS DREAMS

A message for the baker and wine steward

Joseph did well in Egypt – until Potiphar's wife told lies about him, and he was thrown into prison! There he met the king's chief baker and the king's wine steward. They were prisoners too.

One night, they had unusual dreams. Joseph said he would try to help them understand what the dreams meant. The wine steward spoke first:

'I dreamt that there was a grapevine with three branches. The grapes ripened and I squeezed them into the king's cup and gave it to him to drink.'

Joseph said, 'In three days the king will let you out of prison and give you back your old job.'

Next it was the baker's turn: 'I was carrying three bread baskets on my head. In the top basket were all sorts of pastries for the king, and the birds were eating them all up.'

You will need:

Large mixing bowl

Mixing spoon

300gm (11oz) plain flour

300gm (11oz) salt

200ml (7fl oz) water

1 tablespoon oil

Poster paints

Paint brush

Sieve

Baking tray covered with greaseproof paper

Wire cooling rack

Rolling pin, plastic knife to cut and shape the dough

*Adult help with using the oven and baking the dough

1 Sieve the flour and salt into the bowl. Pour in the water, adding a little at a time while stirring the mixture with the spoon. Then add the oil.

2 Knead the mixture together with your fingers until smooth. If the dough is too wet, add more flour and if it is too dry, add a little more water.

Joseph told him: 'In three days the king will let you out of prison, but he will cut off your head.'

The poor baker was very worried.

But it all happened just as Joseph had said.

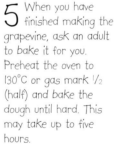

Make this grapevine out of salt dough and paint it to remind you of the wine steward's dream.

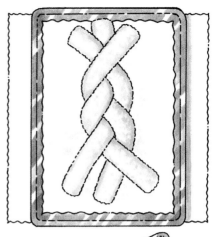

3 Make three long sausage shapes from the dough by rolling it on a flat surface. Place the shapes on the baking tray covered with the greaseproof paper. Twist or plait them together at one end to form the trunk of the vine with three branches.

4 Roll out a piece of dough using the rolling pin and use the plastic knife to cut out some leaf shapes. Place these on the branches. Then make lots of small balls of dough with your fingers and stick these together on the branches to make the bunches of grapes. Brushing water on to the dough will help it stick together.

5 When you have finished making the grapevine, ask an adult to bake it for you. Preheat the oven to 130°C or gas mark 1/2 (half) and bake the dough until hard. This may take up to five hours.

6 Carefully slide the grapevine from the baking tray on to the wire rack to cool. Then paint it with the poster paints.

MOSES IN THE BULRUSHES
The baby in the basket

You will need:

✂

Large sheet of thin white card

Paints and paint brush

Ruler, pencil and scissors

Blunt needle and coloured twine

Clear sticky tape

1 Paint the sheet of card on both sides with a colourful abstract design. Make sure the first side is completely dry before painting the reverse!

2 Measure and mark the card into 3cm wide strips and carefully cut them out. You will need eight strips 30cm long and four strips 42cm long to begin weaving the basket.

Weave this simple basket and imagine baby Moses being hidden inside.

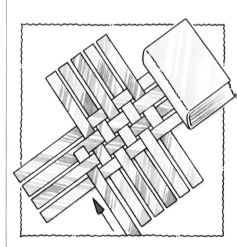

3 Lay the long strips side by side, as shown, and begin to weave the shorter strips in and out to form the base of the basket. Keep all the strips neatly in place. Weight down the long ends with a book to stop them slipping.

Years after Joseph and his family had died, there was a cruel king in Egypt. He had made slaves of God's people and he treated them badly. But there were so many slaves that the king began to fear them.

So he ordered all the baby boys to be thrown into the river and drowned.

But one woman had a clever plan. She hid her baby until he was three months old. Then she made a

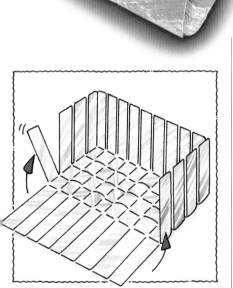

special basket out of reeds and covered it with tar to keep out the water. She put her baby in it and placed it in the bulrushes at the side of the river.

The baby's sister, Miriam, watched close by.

Later the king's daughter came to the river to bathe. She saw the basket, heard a tiny voice and found the baby inside. The princess wanted to help him.

Miriam stepped out from the bulrushes.

'I know who can nurse the baby,' said Miriam. And she fetched her own mother.

The baby was called Moses and was looked after by his mother until he was old enough to live in the royal palace.

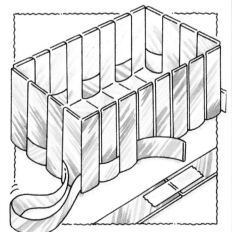

4 Bend up each card strip so it forms a right angle to the base and do this along each side of the basket.

5 Measure and cut three long strips, 3cm wide and 72cm long to weave the sides of the basket. If the strips are not long enough, join two together with clear sticky tape.

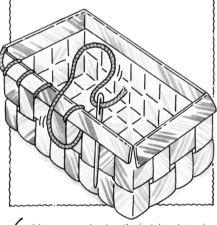

6 Measure and cut a final strip of card 6cm wide and 72cm long. Crease it in half lengthways and fold it over the top edge of the basket. Sew it in place with the coloured twine.

32

THE GOLDEN LAMPSTAND

Light in the tent of meeting

Moses helped to set God's people free when they were slaves in Egypt.

Now God wanted Moses to make special things to go inside the tabernacle or tent of meeting, where God would meet with his people. These were the Covenant Box, which contained the two stone tablets with God's commandments written on them, a table and a lampstand.

The lampstand, the menora, was made of pure gold, with seven branches decorated with golden flowers. The lampstand was very precious. The people brought the best olive oil for the lamp, so that it could be lit each evening. It would burn from evening until morning inside the tent of meeting to help the people remember that God was always with them.

You will need:

Sketching paper and pencil

Wooden beads

Gold poster paint and brush

Dried pasta shapes

Thin knitting needles or wood kebab sticks for painting beads

50cm x 35cm thick cardboard

60cm x 45cm dark blue fabric or paper

PVA glue and brush

Scraps of gold or yellow paper (e.g. sweet wrappers)

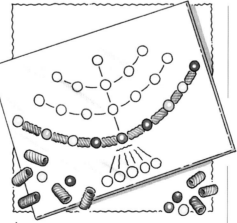

1 First sketch out a simple outline of the lampstand on the paper. Then start to place the pasta shapes and beads over the pencil design.

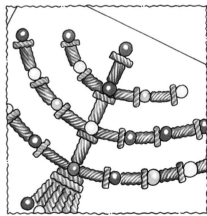

2 When you have finished arranging the pasta and beads, take off all the pieces for painting. Now you will know exactly how many pieces you need to paint.

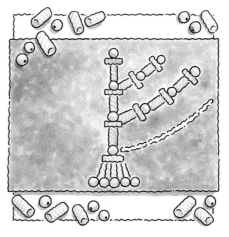

Make this golden lampstand picture and imagine the one in God's tent of meeting.

5 Follow your pencil sketch and begin to arrange the golden pasta shapes and beads on to the backing card. First glue the central stem of the lampstand in place in the middle of the card.

6 Glue all the shapes in place and leave the lampstand picture in a safe place to dry. If you have any scraps of gold or yellow paper, cut out some small flame shapes and glue them above each branch of the lampstand to represent a burning flame.

3 If you thread the beads on to thin knitting needles or wooden kebab sticks, it will make them easier to paint. Pasta absorbs the paint very quickly so it will not take long for the pasta shapes to dry.

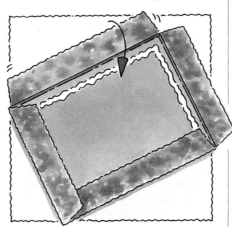

4 Take the piece of thick cardboard and spread the surface with PVA glue. Glue the fabric or paper to the surface, carefully smoothing it flat. Turn the cardboard over and neatly fold and glue the edges of the fabric on to the back.

GIDEON'S VICTORY

'A sword for the Lord and for Gideon!'

Gideon became a leader in Israel. He knew that God was on his side and would help him defeat the Midianite army. He gave each soldier a trumpet and a jar with a burning torch inside.

'This is what we must do,' he told his army. 'When I get to the edge of the camp, watch me and copy what I do. When I blow my trumpet, blow yours too and shout, "A sword for the Lord and for Gideon!"'

So Gideon and his men came to the edge of the camp in the middle of the night. They blew their trumpets and broke the jars they were holding. All the other soldiers did the same.

Everyone broke their jars, picked up their trumpets and shouted: 'A sword for the Lord and for Gideon!'

The enemy army ran away! God had helped Gideon win the battle.

You will need:

✂

Sheets of thin
coloured card and paper
Pencil
Clear sticky tape
Scissors
Length of thick cord
PVA glue and brush
Black felt tipped pen
Coloured string
Paints and brush,
coloured stickers,
stars or shapes
to decorate the trumpet

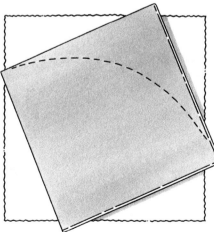

1 Take a square of coloured card and draw a curve across a corner, as shown, then cut off the excess card using the scissors.

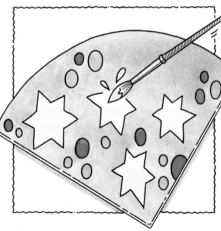

2 If you want to paint the trumpet, it is best to do it while the card is flat. You could also decorate it with coloured shapes and stars, or stickers if you have them.

35

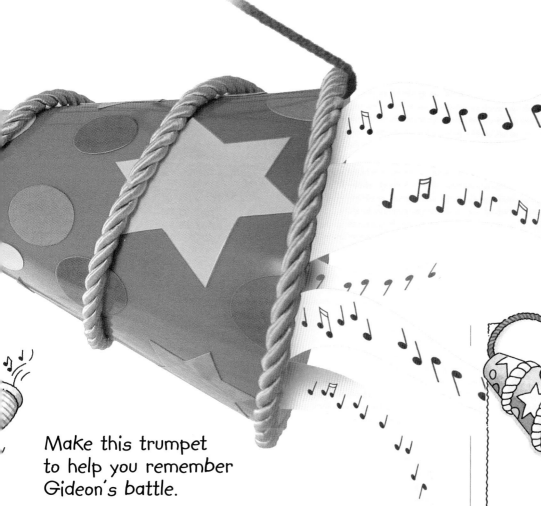

5 When you get to the wide end of the trumpet, glue the cord right around the opening and leave to dry. When it is dry, thread a length of string through the trumpet and tie the ends together. You can hang up the finished trumpet using this string!

Make this trumpet to help you remember Gideon's battle.

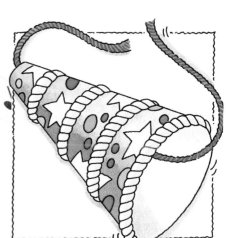

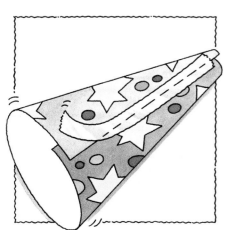

3 Roll the card into a 'trumpet' shape and join the edges together firmly with a length of sticky tape.

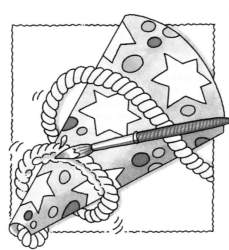

4 Tuck one end of the cord into the hole at the small end of the trumpet and glue in place with PVA glue. Then carefully wrap the cord around the trumpet, gluing it in place as you go with small blobs of PVA.

6 Cut out some long curly shapes from the coloured paper and draw musical notes along the length with the black felt tipped pen. Stick them just inside the trumpet with sticky tape so that they curl out of the opening.

THE STRENGTH OF SAMSON

God's strong man

Samson was a very, very strong man. He once fought a lion and killed it with his own hands! God had made him strong. But nobody knew the secret of his great strength.

One day, Samson met a woman called Delilah. Samson's enemies paid her to find out the secret of his strength. Delilah kept on and on asking him until finally he could stand it no longer.

'If I cut off my hair, I will be made weak,' said Samson.

So when Samson was asleep, Delilah called to his enemies and they cut off his hair. At once his strength left him. He was blinded and thrown into prison in chains.

But Samson's hair began to grow again.

Samson's enemies had a big party in the temple because they had captured Samson. Samson prayed to God to give him his strength back one more time.

With a mighty effort, he pushed over the pillars of the temple.

The roof fell down. Samson died, but he took all his enemies with him.

You will need:

✂

2 x 25cm squares of yellow felt

Black felt tipped pen

Sewing needle and thread

Small scraps of orange, red, light and dark brown, blue and white felt

Scissors

Sketching paper, pencil and tracing paper

Scraps of wool for whiskers

PVA glue in a small plastic bottle with a nozzle, spreader and cocktail stick

Piece of scrap card

1 Place your hand on a piece of yellow felt and use it as a guide to make the 'glove' shape. Draw around your hand with the felt tipped pen and make the shape 2-3cm bigger than the hand. Make sure that your thumb and small finger fit into the two 'arms' of the puppet shape and cut it out.

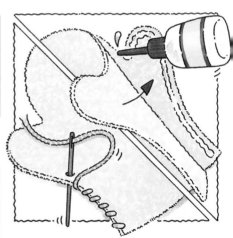

2 Make a second identical felt glove shape and join the two shapes together, leaving the bottom open. Either sew the two pieces together or glue them with PVA, using the nozzle to spread a thin line of glue around the edge of one of the gloves.

3 Sketch out your own lion face design and trace it. Use the tracing to mark out the shapes on different coloured felt and cut them all out.

4 Start by cutting out the mane from brown felt, the face shape from yellow felt and two orange ear shapes. Glue the two ears to the mane, then glue the mane to the top part of the glove and glue the yellow face to the centre of the mane. Place a piece of scrap card inside the glove to prevent glue soaking through to the bottom layer.

5 Carefully cut out the other smaller felt shapes – a brown mouth, two white teeth and large eye circles, two small blue eyes, two fierce brown eyebrows, two orange muzzle shapes, a red tongue and a brown nose. Use a cocktail stick to dab small blobs of PVA on to the shapes and stick them to the face. Begin with the eyes, then the mouth and teeth. Glue the lengths of wool across the face and glue the muzzle and nose over the top.

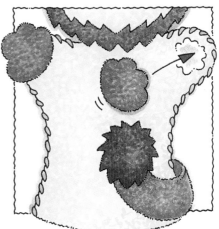

6 Finally cut out a long tail shape from the orange felt. Glue one end to the back of the puppet and the other end to the front. Cut out a shaggy brown felt shape and glue it over the front end of the tail. Cut out two orange paws and glue them to the ends of both arms.

Make this lion glove puppet to remind you of Samson's great strength.

DAVID'S HARP
Music for King Saul

King Saul was a very troubled man. He used to be happy but he had not done what God had told him to do. Now he often sat in his room feeling terrible.

His servants thought that it might help him to listen to some music.

'There is a boy in Bethlehem,' said one servant, 'who is very good at playing the harp. His name is David. He takes care of his father's sheep.'

They told Saul and he asked them to fetch David.

David set off from home with a young goat, a donkey, food and drink.

He went to see the king, ready to play his harp.

King Saul listened to him playing the harp and suddenly felt much better. The music helped him to feel calm again.

'Stay here,' he said to David. 'I wish to hear more.'

So David stayed with King Saul. Whenever the king felt terrible, David would play beautiful music on his harp.

You will need:

Some adult help in cutting the wooden pieces to size and to supervise the construction of the harp. Use sandpaper to smooth any rough edges

Pieces of wood or DIY off-cuts:
24cm x 18cm x 1cm
50cm x 3cm x 1cm
45cm x 3cm x 1cm
40cm x 3cm x 1cm

8 brass eyelets

Nylon fishing line or nylon guitar strings

Tools:
saw, hammer, sandpaper and small nails

Paints, palette and brush

Pencil and ruler

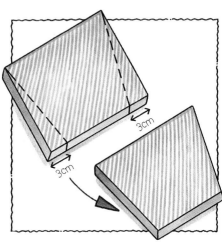

1 Take the rectangle of wood, measure and mark the dimensions as shown, then ask an adult to saw the wood to size. This is the base of the harp and the shape will make the finished harp look more authentic!

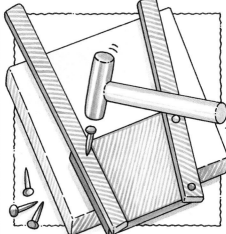

2 Take the two longer lengths of wood and position them on the base as shown, lining up the two ends. Carefully nail into place.

3 Take the cross bar and nail it to the two supports, making sure that the same length of wood overlaps at each end.

4 Now you can paint the harp. Either paint it with bright colours and patterns, or keep the wooden finish of the frame and decorate it with painted patterns.

Make this simple harp to remind you of David playing for the King.

5 Ask an adult to help you screw a row of eyelets into the top of the base. Measure and mark the position of each eyelet with a pencil point to make sure the row is evenly spaced.

6 Use lengths of nylon fishing line or even nylon guitar strings to make strings for the harp. Tie one end of line to each eyelet and wind the other end around the top bar. Keep each line as tight as possible and secure with a knot. You may be able to tighten and 'tune' the strings by twisting the eyelets.

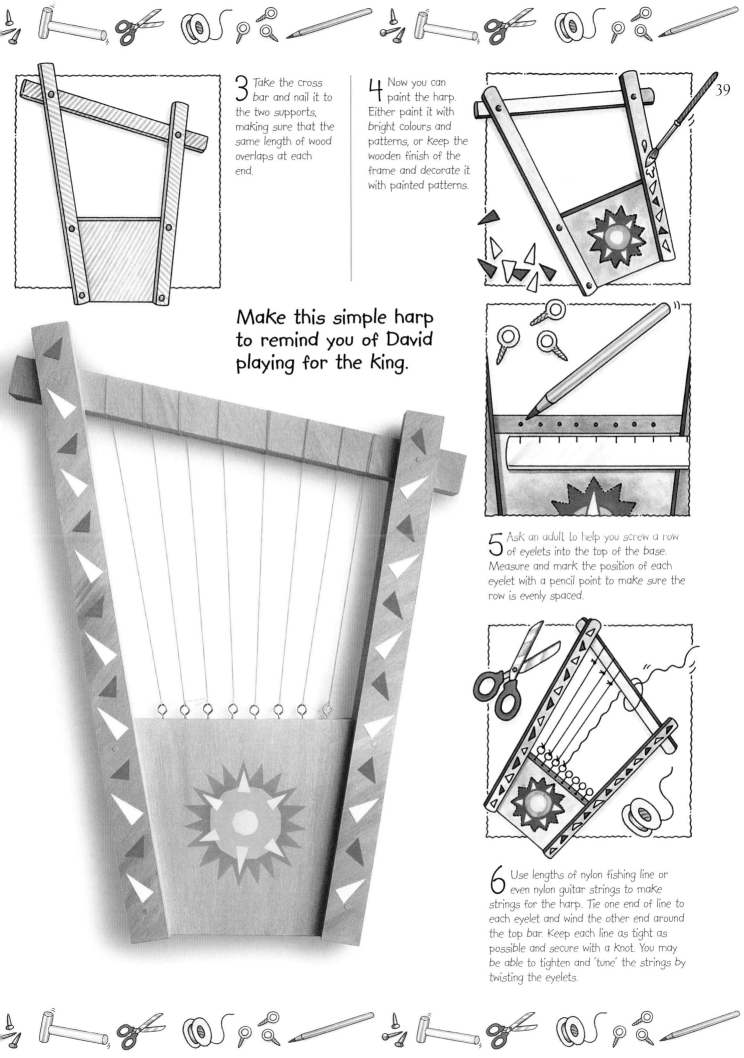

DAVID AND GOLIATH
The shepherd boy and the giant

King Saul had enemies.

Goliath, the champion of the Philistine army, asked King Saul to find a man who would fight him. But Goliath was over three metres tall! Nobody in Saul's army even dared to try!

For forty days, Goliath asked the army, 'Who will fight me?'

Then one day, David left his sheep to take some food to his brothers, who were soldiers in the camp.

David heard Goliath shouting. He couldn't understand why no one stepped forward. David had often fought wild animals to protect his sheep.

'God will help me fight Goliath,' said David, 'as he has helped me protect my sheep.'

'Then put on my armour and take my sword,' King Saul said. But they were much too heavy for David.

David had his own plan. He went to the river and chose five smooth stones. He took out his sling, then set off to face Goliath. With a quick flick of his wrist, he whirled the sling round his head and threw one of the stones at Goliath. It hit him on the forehead and killed the giant!

The Philistines turned and ran away, chased by King Saul's army. God had given the Israelites a victory!

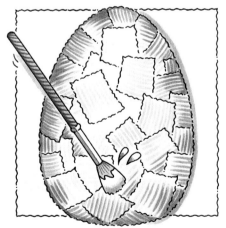

You will need:
✂

Large rounded pebble

Newspaper

PVA glue and brush

Old bowl to mix up the papier mâché

Piece of thick corrugated cardboard

Scissors

Bronze and coloured poster paints and brush

Scraps of felt, string and coloured card for decoration

Small stick

1 Wrap the large pebble with strips of glued newspaper. Build up the newspaper strips until you have a 'body' shape that is flatter at the base with a rounded top. Leave to dry.

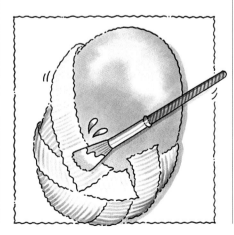

2 Refine the shape by sticking smaller pieces of newspaper to the body. Keep the surface as smooth as possible.

5 Cut two hands from brown felt and glue these to the arms with PVA. Cut strips of felt from another colour to make cuffs and glue them on to hide the joins. Glue finished arms to the body. Then make Goliath's headdress from scraps of orange and blue felt as shown.

3 Cut out the feet shape from the corrugated card. The feet must stick out from under the body when it is placed on top. Glue the body to the feet and build up the shapes of the feet with pieces of papier mâché.

4 When the papier mâché is completely dry, the figure can be painted. Make Goliath's face as fierce as possible and give him a large bushy beard! Cut two arms from felt in a colour to match Goliath's armour.

Use a pebble to make this paperweight and remember how God helped David.

6 Make Goliath's spear from a stick with a card point, attached with string, as shown here. Cut the dagger from coloured card. Glue both to Goliath's hands with PVA.

DANIEL IN THE LIONS' DEN

You will need:

White sketching paper

Ruler

Rolling pin and board

Newspaper

Paints and paint brush

Raffia and large blunt needle

Length of thin elastic

Pencil

Plasticine and cutting tool/blunt knife

Cling film

PVA glue and brush

Scissors

Pipe cleaners

Saved from the mouths of lions

Daniel was taken to live in a country far away from his home. He loved God and prayed to him, but the people around him didn't like it.

Daniel worked hard and the king made him a leader.

But Daniel's enemies were jealous and plotted against him.

The king had made a rule that no one should pray to anyone but the king for thirty days, or they would be thrown into a pit of lions. When Daniel still prayed to God, he was arrested and taken

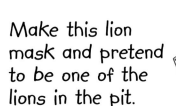

Make this lion mask and pretend to be one of the lions in the pit.

1 First, plan the design for your lion mask. Measure the width of your face and draw a large circle of this diameter. Add simple features: eyes, ears, nose, whiskers and mane.

2 Looking at your sketch, make a simple plasticine mould for the papier mâché mask. Roll out the plasticine to a thickness of 3cm. Cut out a large circle for the face, then triangles for the ears, a wedge shape for the nose, and small circles for the cheeks. Roll out 'sausage' shapes for the eyebrows.

4 Tear up small strips of newspaper. Use a diluted solution of PVA glue to cover the mould with six layers of paper. Make sure each layer covers evenly.

to be fed to the lions!
The king was horrified because Daniel was his friend but he hoped that Daniel would somehow survive.

As soon as morning came, he went back to the lions' pit and called, 'Daniel! Has your God saved you?' Daniel called back, 'Yes! I'm alive!' God had sent an angel to stop the lions from harming him. The king released Daniel and punished the men who had tried to hurt him.

Daniel was free to pray to God for the rest of his life, and the king honoured Daniel's God who had the power to save.

3 Use your shapes to build up the lion's features and make a 3D mould. Then cover the plasticine mould with cling film.

5 Leave the mask to dry. Then carefully pull the layer of cling film away and use it to remove the mask from the mould. Trim around the mask with scissors and cut out the eye holes. Paint the lion mask.

6 Use a sharp pencil to make holes around the mask. Thread the needle with lengths of raffia and sew them through the holes, knotting them at the back. Use the pipe cleaners for whiskers. Make two holes on each side of the mask, thread elastic through and adjust to fit.

44

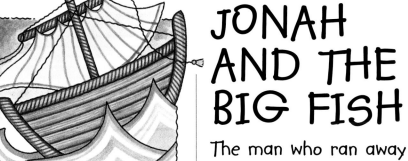

JONAH AND THE BIG FISH

The man who ran away

You will need:

✂

3 sheets of A4 card

Scissors

Paints or colouring pencils

Sharp pencil

5 split pins

String

Weight (e.g. key, large metal washer, or similar)

Ruler

1 Draw an underwater scene on the first sheet of A4 card. This is the background for the picture. Use paints or pencils to colour in the waves and shoals of fish. Then draw a similar watery scene half-way up the second sheet of card and cut it out. This is the foreground strip.

2 On the third sheet of card draw a big fish with a large open mouth, as shown here, and a small figure of Jonah. Use paints or pencils to colour them in, then carefully cut out both shapes.

3 Measure a point in the centre of the fish and make a small hole (X) with a sharp pencil. Measure and mark two more holes (A and B) 4cm either side of X.

God told Jonah to go to Nineveh and tell the people that he was angry with them. Jonah was afraid and ran away from God.

He went aboard a ship and set sail for a distant shore.

God sent a mighty storm and the sailors thought they would all drown.

Jonah told them to throw him into the sea.

The storm stopped as soon as Jonah sank down into the dark water. But God saved Jonah from drowning. He sent an enormous fish to come and swallow up Jonah.

Jonah lived inside the fish for three days and three nights. When the fish spat him out, Jonah did as God had asked him.

The people of Nineveh told God they were sorry and changed their ways. And, because God loved the people he made, he forgave them.

45

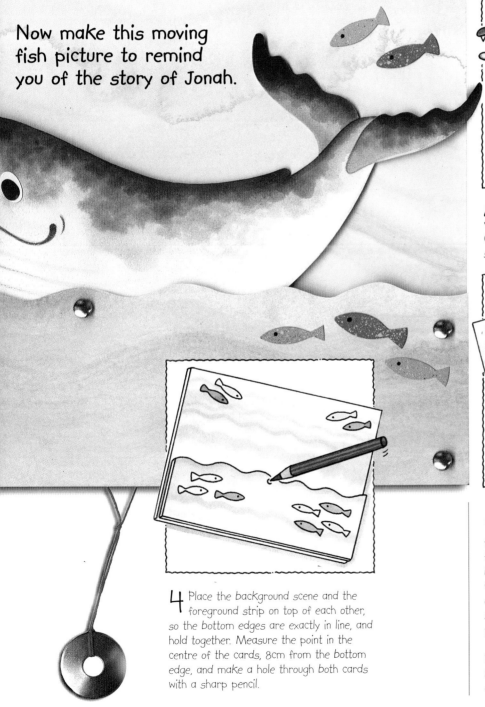

Now make this moving fish picture to remind you of the story of Jonah.

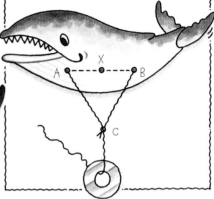

5 Tie a length of string through holes A and B, and knot the strings together at C. Then tie the weight to the ends of the strings.

6 To assemble the picture, push a split pin through the centre hole in the foreground strip, through the hole X in the fish and through the hole in the background. Secure the pin at the back. Glue Jonah to the background, behind the open mouth! Also attach the foreground strip to the background with four split pins.

Pin the picture firmly to a wall or notice board. Swing the weight and watch the fish devour Jonah!

4 Place the background scene and the foreground strip on top of each other, so the bottom edges are exactly in line, and hold together. Measure the point in the centre of the cards, 8cm from the bottom edge, and make a hole through both cards with a sharp pencil.

AN ANGEL VISITS MARY

News of the baby King!

Mary lived in a little town called Nazareth. She was soon to be married to Joseph, the carpenter. But one day she had a visitor with some surprising news which changed Mary's life for ever.

God sent the angel Gabriel to talk to Mary!

'Greetings!' said the angel. 'Don't be afraid. God has chosen you out of all the women in the world. You will have a baby and he will be called God's son. You shall call him Jesus. He will be a king for ever.'

'I am God's servant,' said Mary. 'I will do as God asks.'

The angel left, and Mary sang a song of praise to God for choosing her to be the mother of God's son.

You will need:

✂

A4 coloured card

Glue stick

Ruler, pencil and scissors

Paints and brush

Coloured stickers for decorating the card

Holographic paper

Small length of gold cord and thread

Make this pop-up card as a reminder of Mary's surprise visit from the angel Gabriel.

1 Cut the A4 card in half. Fold one piece in half to make the card. It is easier to decorate the card before sticking in the pop-up, so paint a design on the back and front, or use coloured stickers if you have them.

2 Use the pencil and ruler to draw a strip 15cm x 3cm long on the second piece of card, then cut it out. Fold the strip exactly in half and crease the centre fold. Make two more folds in the strip 2cm from each end as shown.

5 Cut out two wings from holographic paper and an oval shape from plain card for the face. Draw the angel's face on to the oval and glue it to the top of the body. Glue the wings to the back. To make the curly hair take a 10cm piece of gold cord. Tie it firmly in the centre with thread and fray the ends, then glue the hair to the head.

3 Place the strip in the middle of the card so that the creases in the strip and the card match exactly. Keep the strip in this position and stick the two ends to the card with the glue stick.

4 Either paint your pop-up angel or make it from scraps of paper as shown here. Cut out a triangular shape and two arms from the scraps of card you have left. Cover these with small pieces of holographic paper to decorate the angel's robes and glue the arms to the body.

6 When the glue is completely dry, fold the angel in half and make a firm crease along the centre fold. Glue the angel to the pop-up strip, making sure the crease on the strip and the angel's centre fold match up exactly. When you open the card, the angel will pop out.

48

MARY AND JOSEPH TRAVEL TO BETHLEHEM

The rooftops of Bethlehem

1 Make the pockets by folding one of the long strips of felt in half lengthways and pinning together. Mark out twelve pockets by drawing a line with the felt tipped pen at 5cm intervals along the strip.

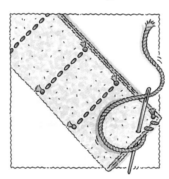

2 Sew along each line with a simple running stitch, knotting the thread at each end on the same side as the felt-tipped pen lines, making this side the back. Oversew each end of the strip. Repeat with the other strip until all twenty-four pockets are done.

3 Spread PVA glue along the back of the first strip of pockets and glue it to the bottom of the piece of blue felt. Then glue the second strip of pockets above the first. This leaves plenty of space above the pockets for the Bethlehem scene.

4 Cut out the shapes to make the felt collage. The buildings are all rectangles. Start by gluing down the large shapes at the back of the town but use the glue sparingly.

You will need:

60cm x 40cm piece of blue felt

Pins, needle and thread

2 strips of coloured felt, 60cm x 10cm

Scissors

Pieces of coloured felt: yellow, green, brown, grey, purple, etc.

PVA glue and spreader

Gold fabric marker pen

Ruler

Coloured braid and sequins for decoration (optional)

Fine felt tipped pen

24 small toys and sweets for the pockets

4 curtain rings

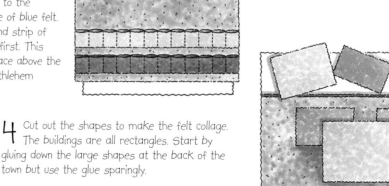

Mary had to wait many months before her baby was ready to be born. During that time, the Roman emperor had ordered a census. Joseph was told that he must go to Bethlehem to be counted.

Mary and Joseph had to travel all the way to Bethlehem on foot. Their donkey carried their clothes, food and a bottle of water. It was a very long, dusty journey. Mary became very tired. She was nearly ready to have her baby and needed to rest often.

'Come on, Mary,' said Joseph gently. 'We will soon see Bethlehem in the distance.'

Suddenly, over the brow of a hill, they could see the rooftops and trees of the little town of Bethlehem. At last they were nearly there!

Count down the days before Christmas with this Advent calendar!

5 Build up the scene, working forward and overlapping the houses. Position the palm trees by gluing the trunks down first, then adding the leaves. Finally, cut out lots of small yellow and orange squares and rectangles to make the lighted windows and doors.

6 Use the gold fabric marker to write the numbers 1 to 24 on each pocket. Add extra decorations and sequins if you have them and sew the curtain rings along the top of the calendar. Here's the fun part! Fill up all the pockets with sweets and small toys and hang up the calendar ready for 1 December.

BETHLEHEM IS FULL

No room at the inn!

You will need:

Rectangles of fabric or felt, approx 26cm x 12cm

Scissors, needle, sewing thread and pins

PVA glue, brush and cocktail sticks as an alternative to sewing

Small scraps of coloured fabric or felt for decoration

Lengths of coloured cord, approx 60cm for each bag

Sequins for decoration

When Mary and Joseph finally arrived in Bethlehem, they were very tired. Mary was getting worried. Her baby was soon going to be born! They needed to find a place to sleep for the night.

Joseph carried their heavy bags and knocked on the door of the inn. But it was already full! So many people had come to Bethlehem to be counted, just like Joseph. Now where could they stay?

The innkeeper saw that Mary was soon going to have a baby. He took pity on her.

'I'm sorry there's no room in my inn,' he said. 'But you are welcome to sleep in the place behind the inn where the animals sleep. At least the straw is dry and you'll be safe for the night.'

'Thank you!' said Joseph. Mary and Joseph and their donkey followed the innkeeper behind the inn. At last Mary could lie down and rest.

1 Fold the rectangle of fabric in half and pin the sides together. Sew along the two sides using small stitches and leave the top open. Alternatively you can glue the two sides together with PVA.

3 Cut out squares from different coloured felt or fabric and glue them in patterns to both sides of the bag. Then sew or glue sequins on to the bag to complete the design.

4 To make the drawstring bag, use the tips of the scissors carefully to snip a row of holes in the bag 3cm from the top. Make the holes about 2cm apart and large enough to thread the cord through.

5 Take a 60cm length of cord, tie knots approximately 3cm from each end and thread the cord in and out through the row of holes in the bag.

6 Cut out some star shapes from coloured felt and glue them around the bag. Then sew or glue sequins on to the bag and around the opening. Fill the bags with sweets or small toys to make really special Christmas gifts.

2 To make the bag with the long cord strap, take the 60cm length of cord and tie a knot approximately 3cm from each end to stop the cord from fraying. Then sew (or glue) the cord along both sides of the bag so the knots are positioned in the two bottom corners of the bag.

Make these special gift bags and remember Mary and Joseph's journey to Bethlehem.

52

JESUS IS BORN
Mary has a baby boy

The time soon came for Mary's baby to be born.

'It's a boy!' shouted Joseph.

'He is called Jesus,' said Mary. The angel Gabriel had told her to give him that special name.

Mary looked lovingly at her tiny firstborn son. He was so precious to her, and so helpless now. But Mary knew that God had a very important plan for his son. He would change the world.

Mary wrapped her baby in cloths and laid him in the soft hay in a manger to sleep.

Make these finger puppets to recreate the wonder of the Christmas story.

You will need:

Scraps of coloured felt and fabric

Scissors and pins

Sewing needle and threads to match the felt

PVA glue, brush and cocktail sticks

Beads and scraps of yarn to decorate the figures

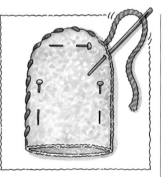

1 Cut out the felt to make Joseph, the shepherds and wise men. You will need two body shapes, arms, headdress, face and beard for each puppet. Pin the two body pieces together and sew around the edge with small stitches, leaving the bottom open. (Alternatively the body pieces could be glued together.)

2 Glue the arms into position across the back. Use the cocktail stick to glue all the other small pieces of felt to the body, dabbing small amounts of PVA glue where it is needed.

3 The head dress is glued in place over the top of the body, then the face and beard. Finally glue the beads to the face, a small stick to a hand and a small piece of thread around the head as a headband. Use different coloured felt for all the men and decorate the wise men's clothes with beads and give them a gift to hold.

5 Cut out all the pieces of felt you need to make the animals. Pin and sew the body pieces together as before. To make the sheep, sew the nose to the face shape and glue two ears to the back of the face, then glue the face to the body.

6 For the donkey and ox, glue their nose shapes, ears and eyes directly on to the bodies. Make their tails and manes from pieces of yarn which you can sew or glue in place.

4 To make Mary, follow the instructions for Joseph but use the needle and red thread to sew the nose and mouth features to the face before gluing the face over the head-dress. To make baby Jesus, use the body shape, but cut 5mm off the length. Cut out and glue on a smaller face and sew two eyes as shown. Cut out a strip of grey felt long enough to wrap round the baby. Glue on, crossing it over the front of the body.

Make these Christmas cards to give to your family and friends.

THE SHEPHERDS' SURPRISE

The angel's good news

You will need:

✂

A4 sheets of coloured card

Small scraps of brown felt

Pieces of black and green paper

Small scraps of white paper (for eyes) or small white stickers

Scissors

White pencil

White tissue paper

Clear sticky tape

Glue stick

Black felt tipped pen

On the hills near Bethlehem, a group of shepherds were looking after their sheep. It was night and they had to make sure that no wild animals came to snatch their sheep away.

The shepherds camped round a fire to keep them warm. They began to feel a bit sleepy.

Suddenly there was a blinding light in the sky. An angel appeared!

'Don't be afraid!' he said. 'I have come to bring you good news. This very night a baby has been born in Bethlehem. He is Christ the Lord! You will find the baby wrapped in strips of cloth and lying in a manger. Go now and see him!'

The shepherds could not speak – they were so frightened and amazed.

Then a whole host of angels appeared in the sky. 'Glory to God in the highest,' they sang, 'and on earth peace to everyone who pleases God!'

It was a beautiful sound.

1 Use the white pencil to draw a simple outline of a sheep on the black paper. Then cut it out carefully with scissors.

2 To make the stand-up card, fold a sheet of A4 card in half and glue the sheep shape to the centre of the card using the glue stick.

3 Tear up small pieces of white tissue paper, roll them into small balls with your fingers and begin to glue them to the body of the sheep. Start around the edge, gluing small areas with the glue stick as you go. Gradually fill in the body shape leaving the black head and legs showing.

4 Cut out two ear shapes from the felt and glue them to the head. Glue more white tissue balls to the top of the head and also make a long curly white tail.

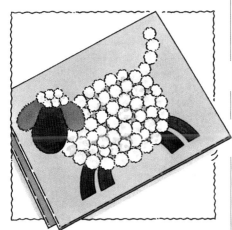

5 Cut a long grassy strip from the green paper and glue it along the bottom of the card. Cut out two white spots for eyes, or use white stickers, and glue them to the face. Make pupils with a black felt tipped pen. You could also glue some stickers to the background as snowflakes.

6 The zig-zag card is made in a similar way. Fold the A4 sheet of card into four as shown. Cut along the long centre fold and across one of the pieces. Then attach the two pieces together as shown with clear sticky tape. Then decorate the card with three sheep.

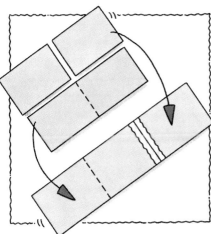

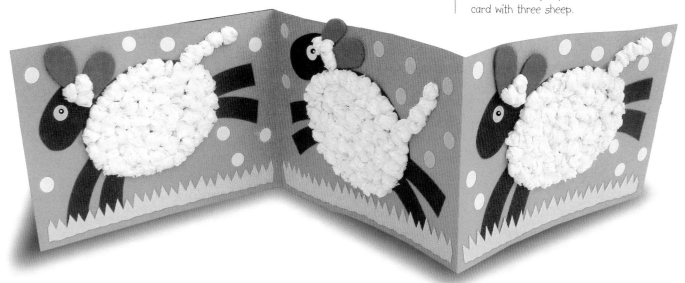

56

SHEPHERDS GO TO FIND JESUS
The baby in the manger

'Hurry, hurry!' shouted the shepherds. 'We must hurry to Bethlehem at once to find the baby which God has told us about!'

They hurried through the town, looking for a newborn baby. They knocked at the door of an inn.

'Is there a baby here?' they asked the innkeeper.

The innkeeper showed the shepherds through to the back of the house, where the animals slept. And here they found Mary and Joseph. There, in a manger, wrapped up in cloths, was the newborn baby: Jesus, their Saviour. The shepherds looked at the tiny baby and they felt great joy in their hearts.

When they had said goodbye, they hurried into the town telling everyone they met, 'We've seen Jesus!'

They danced and sang songs to God, praising him for all they had seen. It had been just as the angel had said.

You will need:

✂

2 x 12cm lengths of thin card tube (fax rolls are ideal, but ask an adult to cut the lengths)

Scissors

4 glittery coloured pipe cleaners

8 bells

2 pieces of Christmas wrapping paper 14cm x 14cm

Glue stick

PVA glue and brush

Lengths of pretty ribbon

Scraps of coloured tissue paper

1 Place the card tube on top of the wrapping paper, leaving 1cm of paper at either end. Use the glue stick to glue the paper to the tube and tuck the excess paper into the ends of the tube.

2 Twist two of the pipe cleaners together to join them and keep twisting for approximately 8cm. Then thread the first bell on to one pipe cleaner and twist the pipe cleaners together again to hold the bell in place.

3 Continue twisting the pipe cleaners together, threading on all four bells at equal distances apart. Finish off twisting the last length of pipe cleaners together.

4 Dab a little PVA glue on to the ends of the pipe cleaners, covering about 5cm at both ends. Push the pipe cleaners into each end of the tube and leave to dry. If the card tube is rather wide, fill any gaps with scrunched up pieces of coloured paper. Dabs of glue will hold it in place.

5 Finally, tie a length of ribbon around the pipe cleaners at either end of the tube, just where they are attached to the tube. Repeat these instructions to make the second set of Christmas bells. Now sing like the shepherds!

Shake these Christmas bells to celebrate the good news that Jesus has been born.

JESUS IS PRESENTED IN THE TEMPLE

The light of the world

When Jesus was eight days old, Mary and Joseph took him to the temple in Jerusalem with two doves as their offering. They wanted to present him to God and say thank you for their new son.

In the temple there was a very old man called Simeon. He had been waiting all his life to see the Saviour whom God had promised to send. God had told Simeon that he would not die until he had seen him.

When Mary and Joseph came near with Jesus, Simeon knew at once that this was the special child he had been waiting all his life to see. He took Jesus in his arms and thanked God.

'Lord God, now I may go in peace for I have seen the Saviour, the one who will bring light to all the people of God.'

Simeon blessed them. He knew that Jesus was a very special baby and would grow up to do great things.

You will need:

3 long craft pipe cleaners

Kitchen towel

Sticky tape

Thick corrugated card

PVA glue and brush

Craft knife and cutting board

Gold poster paint and brush

Lid, approx 8cm diameter

Newspaper

Red candle and scraps of tinsel for decoration

Some adult help with using the craft knife and lighting the candle

SAFETY NOTE: This project is designed to be used as a Christmas table decoration. The candle should always be lit by an adult and should never be left unattended.

1 Take each pipe cleaner and bend both ends into a curly shape. Then firmly twist all the pipe cleaners together in the centre so they hold together and make the legs for the candle holder.

Make this beautiful candle holder to remind you of the light which Jesus brings.

2 Draw a large star shape on to the corrugated card by drawing two overlapping triangles. Ask an adult to help you cut out the star using the craft knife.

3 Cover the pipe cleaners completely with several layers of glued strips of kitchen towel. This can get messy so cover the surface you are using with plenty of newspaper. Use the glue sparingly and let it dry in between layers.

4 Cover one side of the star with glued kitchen towel to give it a textured finish. Leave to dry, then cover the other side.

5 Place the star on a flat surface and position the pipe cleaners on top. Hold them in place with sticky tape and continue to apply the pieces of glued kitchen towel to secure the pipe cleaner legs firmly to the star. When the legs are dry they should be perfectly rigid and should support the star structure when turned the right way round.

6 Glue the lid to the centre of the star and cover with the glued kitchen towel. When you are happy that the candle holder is completely covered with the textured effect, leave to dry and paint it gold. Place the candle in the holder and wrap a small piece of tinsel or other small decorations around the centre of the holder.

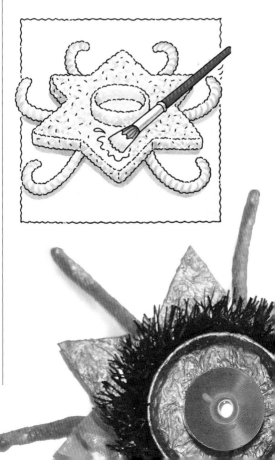

A NEW STAR IN THE SKY

The journey of the wise men

When Jesus was born, some wise men in the east were looking at the stars. They noticed a very bright new star in the sky and were very excited.

'Look at that!' said one of the wise men. 'A new king must have been born!'

So the wise men decided to set off to follow the star.

They took with them fine gifts for the new king.

They followed the star by day and by night, over deserts and hills.

Where would they find the king?

Use the star instructions on page 18 or draw your own star designs with a black felt tipped pen on to a sheet of white paper. When you place the coloured paper over the stars you will be able to see the outlines through the thin tissue.

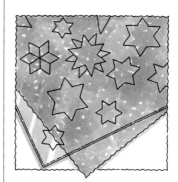

You will need:

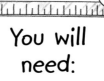

Pack of coloured tissue paper
or
coloured handmade papers

Gold or silver relief fabric paint,
or
gold felt tipped or glitter pens

Coloured A4 card

Scissors

Glue stick

Black felt tipped pen and white paper (optional)

Plain ribbon approximately 5cm wide

Use this star paper for your Christmas gifts.

2 Carefully trace the star shapes on to the paper with the gold pen or fabric paint. Trace as many stars as you can, drawing them all over the sheet. Draw a few test stars to see how long they take to dry. The paint must dry before moving on, otherwise the stars will smudge!

4 Overlap several pieces of torn paper to make your design. The papers are very thin so colours underneath will show through. Draw patterns and squiggles on the card with the gold pen to complete the design.

3 To make a card, first fold a piece of coloured A4 card in half. Tear the paper around the star designs, leaving the uneven torn edges. Glue the back of the paper stars with the glue stick and stick them to the card. The paper is very delicate so use the glue stick carefully.

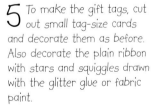

5 To make the gift tags, cut out small tag-size cards and decorate them as before. Also decorate the plain ribbon with stars and squiggles drawn with the glitter glue or fabric paint.

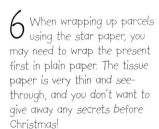

6 When wrapping up parcels using the star paper, you may need to wrap the present first in plain paper. The tissue paper is very thin and see-through, and you don't want to give away any secrets before Christmas!

You will need:

✂

Some adult help with measuring and preparing the ingredients and utensils so everything is ready before you start!

Adult help with handling the tray of cookies in and out of the oven, preheated to 180°C/350°F or Gas mark 4

110g (4oz) butter

275g (10oz) plain flour

110g (4oz) brown sugar

1 teaspoon baking powder

75g (3oz) golden syrup

2 teaspoons ground ginger

1 medium egg

1 teaspoon cinnamon

110g (4oz) sifted icing sugar

1 tablespoon water

Food colours, silver balls and ribbon or cord for decoration

Wooden spoon and mixing bowl

Rolling pin

Greased baking tray

Wire cooling tray

Dessert spoon

Cookie cutters

Plastic straw

GIFTS FOR THE BABY KING

The wise men worship Jesus

The wise men set off towards Bethlehem. The star seemed to stop above a small house in the town.

They knocked on the door and went inside. There they found Mary, with Jesus on her knee. This was the new king they had travelled so far to see!

The wise men bowed down low and worshipped Jesus.

They gave him their fine gifts of gold, frankincense and myrrh. Mary watched in wonder.

God warned the wise men in a dream not to return to Herod's palace. And Joseph too was warned by God to take Mary and Jesus to Egypt, where they would be safe from cruel King Herod.

Make these delicious cookies to share at Christmas.

1 Cream the butter and sugar together in a bowl using the wooden spoon. Add the golden syrup and the egg, and mix until smooth.

2 Sift the flour, baking powder and spices and fold them in to the mixture to form a stiff dough. Shape the dough into a ball and leave it in a cool place or the fridge for at least one hour.

3 Turn the dough on to a floured surface and roll out to 3mm thick. Use the cookie cutters to cut out the shapes and, using a plastic straw, make a hole in some of the cookies to hang on the tree. This quantity of dough will make approximately eight large cookies plus twenty small ones.

4 Place the cookies on a greased baking tray and ask an adult to put them in a preheated oven to bake for 10-15 minutes, or until golden brown. Then leave them to cool on a wire tray.

5 To make the icing, gradually stir the water into the icing sugar until the icing is smooth and firm. If you want coloured icing, add a few drops of food colouring.

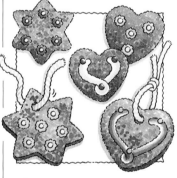

6 Decorate the cookies with the icing and silver balls and leave to dry. Thread ribbon through the holes of some of the cookies and hang them on the tree. The other cookies can be wrapped up and given as special Christmas presents or shared when visitors come.

THE CHRISTMAS STORY

A very special baby

All that had happened that first Christmas had been planned by God long ago.

Then God sent an angel to tell Mary that she would have a baby called Jesus.

'Jesus will be very important: the Son of God and a king!'

Jesus had been born in Bethlehem, and laid in a manger on the soft hay, because there was nowhere to stay at the inn.

God sent angels with a message for the shepherds near Bethlehem so they would know Jesus was the promised Saviour.

Wise men came from the east to visit Jesus, following a very bright star. When they found Jesus, they gave him special presents of gold, frankincense and myrrh. Even their gifts showed that Jesus was no ordinary baby. He would grow up to teach people how much God loved them and how to live the way he wanted them to. But Jesus was also God's son. There were special plans not only for his birth but for his life and death too.

You will need:

✂

White pencil
Dark coloured card
Scissors
Single hole punch
Clear coloured
sweet wrappers
Glue stick
Gold thread
Large blunt needle

1 Use the white pencil to draw a simple animal shape on to the card. Then cut out the shape.

2 Draw star shapes on the card animal and carefully cut them out using the scissors.

3 You can also make patterns of holes in the animal by using a single hole punch.

5 Use the needle to make a hole at the top of the animal and thread a length of gold thread through the hole. Hang the animal up at a window so that light shines through the coloured patterns.

4 Turn the animal shape over. Cut out small pieces of sweet wrapper and stick them over the cut-out shapes with dabs of glue.

Make these Christmas decorations to celebrate the birth of Jesus.

JESUS IS BAPTISED
John baptises Jesus in the River Jordan

There was a man called John the Baptist who talked to people about God. He told them to say sorry for the wrong things they had done. Then John baptised them in the water of the River Jordan as a sign of God washing their sins away.

One day, Jesus came down to the bank of the river to see John.

'I want you to baptise me in the river,' said Jesus.

John was very surprised. He knew that Jesus was very special, and that he had come to show people God's love. But he also knew that Jesus had done nothing wrong and didn't need to be baptised.

When Jesus came out of the river, he saw a dove, and a voice from heaven said, 'This is my son, with whom I am pleased.' It was God's voice speaking.

You will need:

✄

Pale coloured card
Dark coloured card
Pencil
Scissors
Craft knife and cutting mat
Glue stick
Sequins
Coloured felt tipped pens
Elastic

1 Draw a simple dove shape on the pale card and cut it out carefully.

2 Draw a wing shape on the pale card, cut it out and use it as a template to make two more shapes for the second wing and the tail.

3 Decorate the wings and the tail with feather shapes cut from dark card and decorate with sequins. Glue them in place with the glue stick.

4 Ask an adult to cut slots in the middle of the dove's body and by the tail with the craft knife. Decorate both sides of the body with sequins.

5 Cut a strip of light card wide enough to fit through the centre slot and glue a wing shape to both sides of the card strip. Make a small cut in the tail shape and slot it into the body.

6 Use the felt tipped pens to colour in the dove's beak and eyes or glue a triangle of darker card over the beak area. Make a small hole in the top of the dove and thread through a length of elastic, tying it firmly.

Make this decoration of a dove and hang it near a window.

68

TEMPTATION IN THE WILDERNESS
Forty days and forty nights

After Jesus was baptised, he went into the wilderness and ate nothing for forty days and nights. When he was very hungry, the devil came and tempted him to misuse his power.

First, the devil tried to persuade Jesus to turn stones into bread to ease his hunger.

Second, Jesus was taken to the top of the temple and told to throw himself off. 'Don't the scriptures say that the angels will catch you?' said the devil.

You will need:

✂

Empty sweet or crisp box with plastic lid

Craft knife (and some adult help)

Poster paints and brush

Pencil

A4 sheets of green paper

Disc of blue coloured paper (optional)

Scissors

3 craft pipe cleaners

PVA glue in bottle with nozzle

Brown yarn

1 Turn the box upside down so the plastic lid becomes the base, then ask an adult to help you make the slot near the top of the box using the craft knife. Make the slot big enough to take the largest coins.

2 Paint the box with a desert scene of blue sky and golden sand dunes. Paint the top of the box, or glue on a disc of coloured paper.

3 To make the palm trees that decorate the box, first draw six leaves for each tree on the green paper. Cut them out carefully.

4 Position the six leaves together in a bunch as shown. Fold the pipe cleaner in half and twist it around the stem to secure the leaves. Continue twisting the pipe cleaner to make the tree trunk.

Lastly, the devil offered Jesus kingship over all the earth if he would only bow down and worship him.

But Jesus did not give in to any of the temptations. He used passages from the scriptures to show the devil he was wrong to tempt him.

At the end of this time, Jesus was ready to show those around him how to live the way God wanted them to.

Make this money box to help save money and give the money to a charity.

5 Cover the pipe cleaner with lengths of brown yarn by wrapping it around the trunk and gluing it in place.

6 Repeat these instructions to make two more palm trees and use the PVA glue to glue them in place around the money box. It may help to glue one palm tree to the money box at a time, letting it dry before gluing the others in place. Use the money box to save money during Lent so you can give it to a good cause. Empty the box by carefully removing the plastic lid at the base.

THE WEDDING AT CANA

Water into wine

Jesus was once a guest at a wedding in Cana. There was a great feast and everyone was enjoying the party when suddenly the wine began to run out.

'You must do something,' said Mary, Jesus' mother. But Jesus knew what God wanted him to do.

He told the servants to fill six large stone jars with water, then take them to the man in charge of the feast. When the man tasted it, he was very pleased.

You will need:

Thick, pliable cardboard

Pencil and ruler

Craft knife and cutting board

4 cocktail sticks

Small bells, metal buttons, washers, keys

8 beads

Sticky tape

PVA glue, brush and small bowl

Newspaper

Poster paints and brushes

Blu-tack®

Ribbons for decoration

Varnish

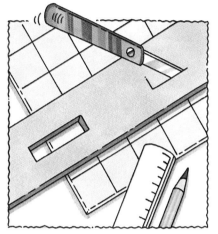

1 With an adult's help, use the craft knife and cutting board to cut a length of cardboard approximately 40cm x 8cm. Mark four evenly spaced holes on the card with a pencil and cut them out.

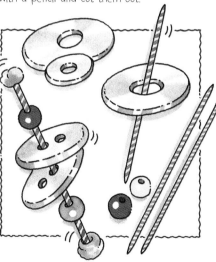

2 Make jingles from any metallic objects such as buttons, washers, keys and bells. Thread them on to cocktail sticks separated with beads and hold in place with Blu-tack®.

'That's funny!' said the man. 'Usually people serve the best wine first, but you have left the best wine till last!' He didn't know that Jesus had done something amazing. Jesus had turned the water into wine.

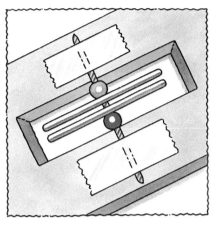

3 Place each threaded stick over a hole, being careful not to dislodge the beads and jingles. Tape them securely into position with small lengths of sticky tape.

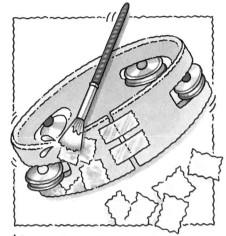

4 Curve the cardboard into the shape of a tambourine and tape the ends together. Then cover the card with pieces of newspaper soaked in PVA glue.

Make this tambourine and imagine you are dancing at a wedding feast.

5 Cover the whole tambourine with several layers of glued paper to strengthen it. Make sure you glue around the holes neatly with smaller pieces of newspaper.

6 Leave the tambourine to dry out completely before painting. Decorate it with bright coloured patterns and, when the paint is dry, give it a coat of varnish. Finally, thread lengths of ribbon through the holes and tie on extra bells if you have them.

THE ARMY OFFICER'S SERVANT

Jesus helps a Roman officer

Jesus healed many people and crowds followed him everywhere.

One day a Roman officer begged Jesus for help.

'My servant is very ill and cannot move.'

Jesus replied, 'I will go and make him well.'

'No, no,' said the officer. 'I know that if you just say the word, he will be healed. I trust that you will heal him.'

Jesus was surprised to hear this and was pleased to find that the officer trusted him.

'Go home, then,' said Jesus. 'What you believe will be done.'

The officer ran home and found to his great joy that his servant had been made well again!

You will need:

✂

Blown-up balloon

Newspaper

PVA glue and brush

Thin card

Scissors

Plastic bowl

Silver and black poster paints

Paint brush

Sharp pencil

Thick string or cord

Split pins

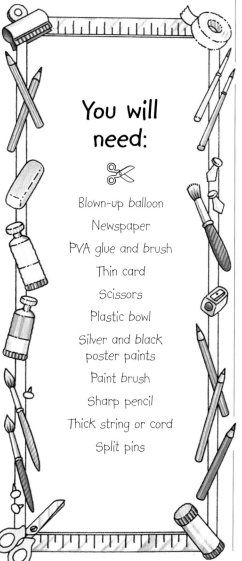

Make this Roman army helmet, similar to that worn by the Roman officer.

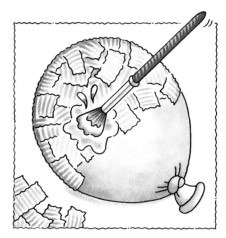

To make the helmet shape, glue torn pieces of newspaper over the top half of the balloon using the PVA glue. Cover the balloon with three more layers and leave to dry.

73

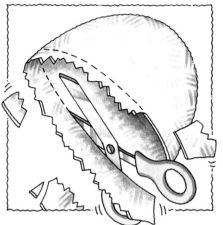

2 Pop the balloon. Then use the scissors to cut off the uneven edge of paper. You will now have the shape that forms the top part of the helmet.

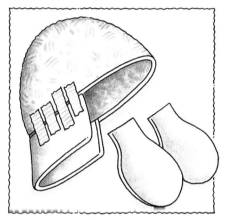

3 Cut out a collar shape and two ear protector shapes from the thin card. The collar will be attached to the back of the helmet. Hold the shapes up to the helmet to make sure you have the correct sizes. Then attach them with glued strips of paper.

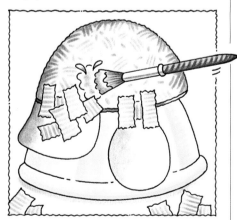

4 It may help to support the helmet over a plastic bowl while you work. Continue to cover the helmet and card shapes with three more layers of glued newspaper pieces, then leave to dry.

5 Wind and glue a length of string around the brim of the helmet. Attach split pins to look like rivets. To attach the pins, first make a hole in the helmet with a sharp pencil point. Push the pin through and cover the splayed ends with pieces of glued newspaper.

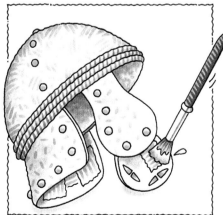

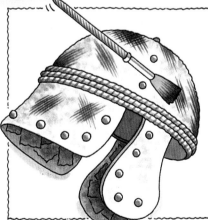

6 Paint the helmet with silver poster paint, making sure that the paint covers all the string and split pins. To give the helmet a tarnished metallic look, mix some black paint with the silver and brush this sparingly over the silver surface. You could also paint inside the helmet with the black paint. Make sure the paint is dry before trying it on!

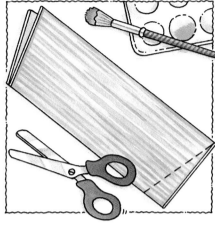

THE STORM ON THE LAKE

Jesus amazes his friends

One day Jesus and his friends got into a boat on the lake.

Suddenly a fierce storm blew up and the boat was tossed about like a cork.

Jesus was fast asleep in the boat, but his friends were terrified of sinking.

'Save us, Lord!' they shouted to Jesus.

'Why are you so afraid?' said Jesus.

Then Jesus got up and ordered the wind and the waves to calm down.

The storm vanished. Everyone was amazed!

'Even the winds and the waves obey him!' they said.

Jesus had saved them all from the storm.

1 Paint the 30cm x 20cm card to look like the wooden hull of a boat and leave to dry. Fold the card in half lengthways. Draw a curve at each end and trim with scissors.

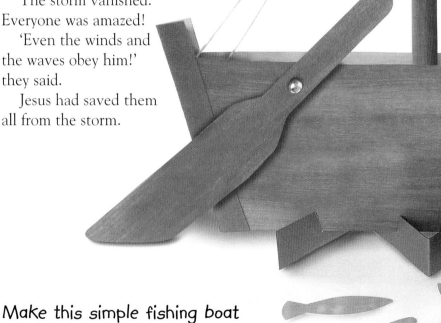

You will need:

- 30cm x 20cm piece of brown card
- Paints and brush
- Scraps of brown card
- Scissors
- PVA glue and brush
- Craft knife and cutting board
- Pencil and ruler
- Thread for rigging
- Square of fabric 20cm x 20cm
- 2 x 25cm dowels
- Scraps of netting and shiny paper fishes
- Split pin
- Narrow strip of card, folded into a zigzag shape, with slots cut into it

Make this simple fishing boat and think about Jesus' power over the storm on the lake.

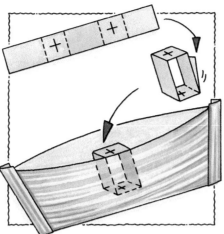

2 Cut two lengths of card 4cm wide and 13cm long. Paint them to look like wood and leave to dry. Fold each piece in half lengthways and glue to each end of the hull.

3 To make the mast support, cut a strip of card 3cm x 20cm and divide it into sections as shown. Cut a cross shape in the two smaller sections with the craft knife and fold the strip along the dotted lines. Glue the support into the centre of the hull.

5 Loosely roll up the sail and tie it to the top of the mast. Then slot the mast into the mast support.

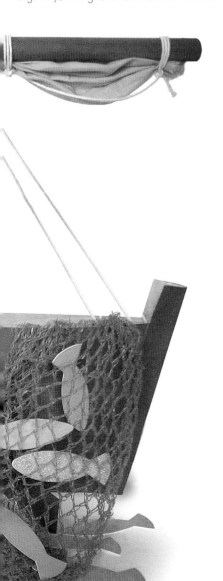

4 Glue the two dowels together with PVA as shown and tie them with thread for extra strength. Brush a thin line of glue across the top of the sail fabric, place the horizontal dowel on top and leave to dry.

6 Cut out a rudder shape from the card and paint it to look like wood. Attach it to the side of the boat with a split pin. To make the boat look more realistic, use the thread to add extra rigging. If you have any netting drape it over the side with a full catch of paper fish!

NB: Because the model boat has a sharp edged bottom, it will need to be propped up or slotted into a zig-zag shape of stiff card. Cut four slots for the boat to stand up in as in main photograph.

76

LOAVES AND FISHES
Jesus feeds more than five thousand people!

Jesus was once speaking to a large crowd of people. There were men, women and even children. They had been listening to him all day and were getting hungry.

Jesus' friends thought the people should go away and buy some food, but Jesus wanted to feed them.

'What food have you got?' he asked his friends.

'Only five loaves and two fishes,' they replied.

Jesus then did something amazing! He shared out the food amongst everyone!

No one went away hungry. Jesus gave them all enough to eat, and there were twelve baskets full of left-overs.

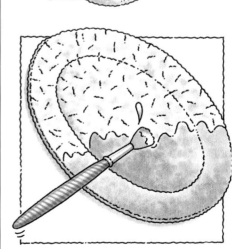

You will need:

✂

Oval plastic plate

Newspaper

Grey paint and paint brush

Pencil

Varnish (optional)

Cooking oil and cling film

PVA glue and brush

Scissors

Coloured magazine pictures

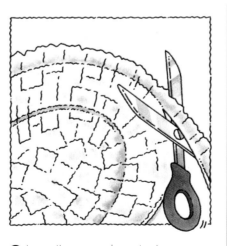

1 Use the plastic plate as a mould. Lightly grease the plate with cooking oil and cover with cling film. Then cover the plate with six layers of newspaper strips, glued with diluted PVA. This will form the plaque for your mosaic.

2 Leave the paper plaque to dry overnight, then remove it from the plate by pulling away the cling film. Neaten the plaque by trimming around the edge with scissors.

3 Choose a neutral grey colour to paint the plaque. This will be the base colour of your fish mosaic.

This beautiful mosaic fish will remind you of how Jesus fed the people.

4 Sketch the outline of the fish design on to the plaque with a pencil. Add in details like the eye, fins and tail, and make a border round the edge of the plaque.

5 Cut out squares of coloured paper from magazine pictures. Arrange the paper squares into groups of similar colours.

6 Follow the pencil lines of the fish, and glue the squares to the plaque with PVA. Build up the mosaic pattern, overlapping the squares if necessary. Finally, you could varnish the finished plaque to strengthen and protect the mosaic.

THE GOOD SEED
The parable of the sower

Jesus told this story to a large crowd beside Lake Galilee.

'Listen! There was once a man who went to sow some corn.

Some of the seed fell along the path where birds came and ate it.

Some of the seed fell on rocky ground where the corn could not grow.

Some of the seed fell among thorn bushes, which choked the plants.

But some of the seed fell in good soil. The plants grew and produced fine corn and there was a good harvest.'

What did the story mean?

God is the sower. The seed is his message. Some people hear God's message but forget about him. Some people try to follow God but give up when trouble comes their way. Some people become too busy with worries, money and all kinds of other things.

But other people are like the seed in good soil; they hear God's message, follow God and live for him.

You will need:

✂

Pencil

Sheet of coloured thick card

Scissors

PVA glue (in a plastic bottle with a nozzle)

Glue spreader or brush

Collage materials: dried seeds, beans, lentils, split peas, pulses

Dried grasses and stems of wheat

1 First you will need to sketch out the design of the collage on the coloured card. Draw the outline of the bird flying over the cornfield. Draw a patterned border around the edge of the card.

2 If you need to, use the scissors to trim the card to the correct size for your design. This will give you guidelines when you start assembling the collage.

3 Begin with the main shapes. Spread the glue along the outline of the bird and press the beans into the glue. Work around the edge of the flying bird first and then fill in the rest of the body.

Make this beautiful collage using dried seeds, pulses and grasses.

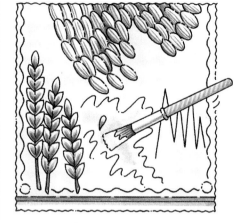

4 Spread PVA glue carefully over the bottom section of the background card which shows the cornfield. Begin to glue the dried grasses and stems of wheat into place.

5 Spread a thin line of glue along the four sides of the card and press a row of beans around the edge to make the border pattern. Put small blobs of glue over the background sky and glue small seeds in place. The PVA glue will dry clear so there shouldn't be any glue showing when your collage is finished.

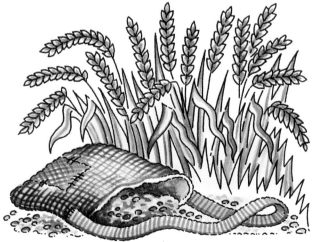

HIDDEN TREASURE

Something worth having

Jesus once told this story:

'A man found some treasure hidden in a field. It was beautiful! It sparkled in the sunlight and the man wanted to keep it.

He went away and sold everything that he had. With the money he got, he bought the field with the treasure in it. Now the treasure belonged to him! He was really happy!'

Jesus often told people stories like this to teach them more about God. He wanted them to think about how important it was to live for God. Jesus told them that, like the hidden treasure in the field, belonging to God is worth more than anything else in the world.

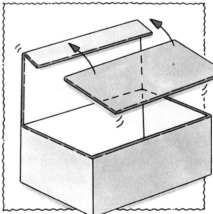

You will need:

Cardboard box with an attached lid

Sheet of thin card

Ruler, pencil and scissors

Sticky tape

Kitchen towel

PVA glue and brush

Lengths of string or cord

Gold poster paint and brush

Selection of buttons, beads, pasta shapes and 'jewels'

2 cocktail sticks

4 small bottle tops (for the legs)

Use the ruler and pencil to measure a 2-3cm strip along the lid of the box and fold this over. Measure the top of the lid and cut out an identical piece from the card. Tape it to the fold along the long sides.

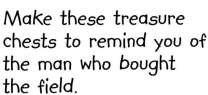

Make these treasure chests to remind you of the man who bought the field.

3 Brush over a small part of the box with PVA glue. Tear up small pieces of kitchen towel and begin to stick them to the surface. Make sure the glued paper stays nice and crinkly. Continue to glue the kitchen towel all over the surface of the box and legs.

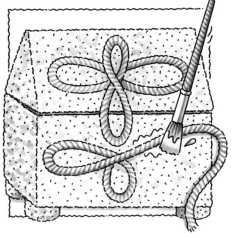

5 Glue lengths of string on to the box making curly patterns. Make an extra long loop on the lid and thread a large bead through the centre of the chest to make the fastening. Also glue string around the rim of the open box. Don't worry if the glue looks a bit messy – you won't be able to see it after the chest is painted!

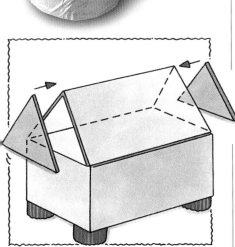

2 Measure two triangular shapes of card to fit exactly at each end of the lid. Cut them out and tape them to both ends of the lid to make the chest's new shaped lid. Glue four bottle tops to the base to make the chest's legs and stand the chest on the legs until they have stuck firmly.

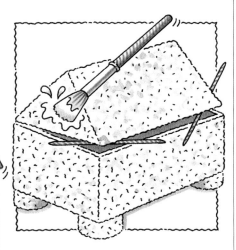

4 Glue a layer of paper over the hinge of the lid, but be careful not to glue the lid to the box – put a couple of cocktail sticks across the opening to keep it apart. Leave the box to dry and then glue a layer of paper on the inside.

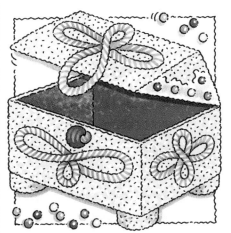

6 If you have any odd coloured buttons or pasta shapes to use as decoration glue them on to the chest before painting it. Then paint the chest in gold paint. Finally, glue on any colourful 'jewels' and beads to make the treasure chest really sparkle!

82

THE WISE AND FOOLISH GIRLS

Are you ready?

You will need:

✂

Self-hardening clay

Tea light candle

Plastic carving tools
and plastic knife to shape
and cut the clay

Small sponge
and water

Paints
and varnish

Jesus once told a story about ten girls at a wedding:

'There were once ten girls who were supposed to meet the bridegroom on his way to the wedding. They carried oil lamps to light the way. But the oil didn't last long in the lamps.

Five of the girls remembered to bring some extra oil with them. But the other five had forgotten. Their lamps went out and they had to run off to buy some more.

While they were away, the bridegroom arrived. The five girls whose lamps were burning brightly met him and went with him to the wedding. The door was shut.

When the other five girls finally arrived, they were too late for the wedding!'

Take a piece of self-hardening clay and knead it in your hands until it is soft. Make a circle of clay roughly 1cm thick and 10cm across. This will be the base of the lamp.

Make this lamp out of clay and imagine you are going to the wedding.

2 Place the tea light candle in the centre of the base. Use small pieces of clay to build up the sides of the lamp, keeping the candle in place in the centre.

SAFETY NOTE:

The clay lamp is designed to hold a tea light candle in a safe way. However, it should not be lit without adult supervision or left unattended.

3 Mould the shape of the lamp with your fingers. Moisten the surface of the clay with a damp sponge to make it easier to work and shape.

5 Continue to smooth the sides and top of the lamp, using your fingers. Make the shape of a spout by pinching in the side of the lamp opposite the handle. Keeping the clay damp makes it easier to smooth the surface.

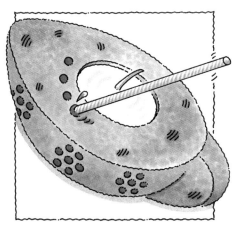

4 Make a handle for the lamp from a piece of clay. Wet the side of the lamp and attach the handle, then smooth over the joins with the tools and the damp sponge.

6 Make some simple patterns on the lamp using the tools and leave to dry. The lamp can be left in its natural clay finish or it could be varnished and painted.

THE LOST COIN

Special to God

Make this coin necklace with card medallions.

You will need:

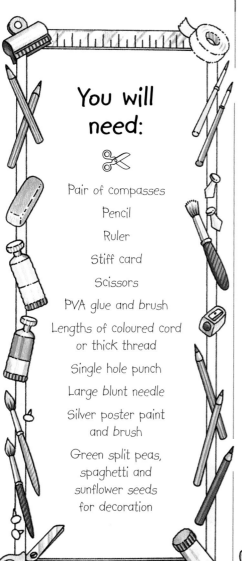

✂

Pair of compasses

Pencil

Ruler

Stiff card

Scissors

PVA glue and brush

Lengths of coloured cord or thick thread

Single hole punch

Large blunt needle

Silver poster paint and brush

Green split peas, spaghetti and sunflower seeds for decoration

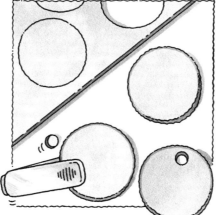

1 Use the compasses to draw ten circles on the card, each with a diameter of 5cm. Cut them out neatly with the scissors. Use the single hole punch to make a hole in each circle.

2 Brush PVA glue on to each circle and use the dried peas, seeds and pieces of spaghetti to make patterns in the centre of each circle. These shapes will make an attractive raised design on each coin, so don't worry about extra blobs of glue!

One day, Jesus told a story about a woman who had lost a special coin:
'A woman had ten silver coins. She lost one and tried hard to find it.
She lit a lamp, swept her house and looked everywhere for it.
Suddenly she found it! There it was, glinting in the
sunlight.

The woman called her friends and neighbours
and said, "Let's have a party! I am so happy to have
found my lost coin!"

In the same way, God is happy when
anybody turns to follow him.'

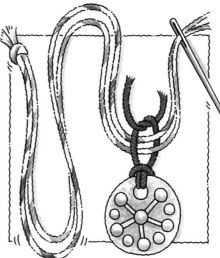

3 When all the textures are firmly glued
in place and the glue is dry, paint the
coins on both sides with silver poster paint
and leave to dry.

5 Cut two or three lengths of coloured
thread, about 80cm long and knot them
together at one end. Tie the coins on to the
thread.

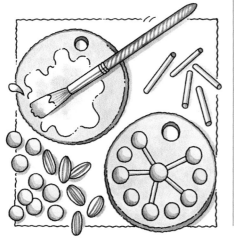

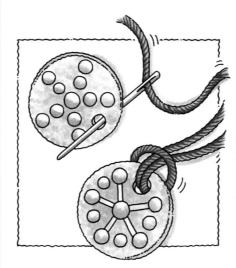

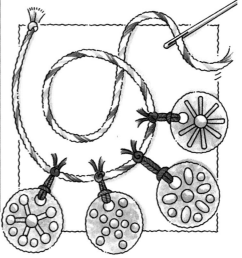

4 Thread the needle with a 12cm length
of thread. Pass it through the hole in
the first coin and loop the thread around
the hole. Then repeat this for all ten coins.

6 Place the finished necklace around
your neck, tie the two ends together
and cut off any surplus lengths. You could
experiment by making other necklaces with
lots more coins decorated with different
textures.

JESUS ENTERS JERUSALEM

You will need:

Lengths of fabric approx. 20cm wide

PVA glue and brush

Pins, sewing needle and thread

Paints and brush

Small scraps of multicoloured fabric or felt

Coloured sticky tape

2 dowel rods or bamboo canes

Plasticine balls

Trimmings: buttons and beads

Scissors

Coloured yarn, card and scissors for tassel making

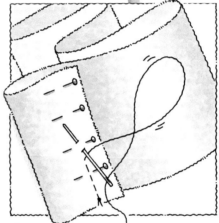

1 Cut a long length of fabric 20cm wide. You can make the banner as long as you like! Turn a 3cm strip of fabric over at each end, pin in place and sew into position. These form the slots for the dowels.

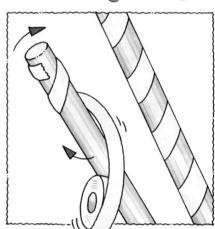

2 Give each dowel a coat of paint and leave to dry. Attach the coloured tape to the top of the dowel, then slowly twist the dowel, sticking the tape firmly to the dowel as it's turning. This gives the dowels an attractive diagonal pattern.

Welcome the King!

Clip, clop, went the donkey's hooves on the road.
'Hosanna! Hurray!' shouted the crowd.
    Who was this, riding on a donkey? It was Jesus!

The people were so excited to see him.
They threw down cloaks in front of the donkey
and waved palm branches in the air.
    'God bless the king!' they shouted.
Jesus was welcomed into the city.

Make this simple banner to wave and think of the crowd cheering for Jesus.

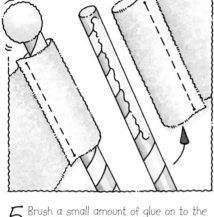

5 Brush a small amount of glue on to the dowels, covering 15cm from the top, then carefully push them into the slots at each end of the banner. When the glue is dry, push the plasticine balls on to the top end of each dowel.

3 Use the fabric scraps to decorate the banner. Cut out flowers and animal shapes and arrange them along the length of fabric. Start to glue down the shapes when you are happy with your design.

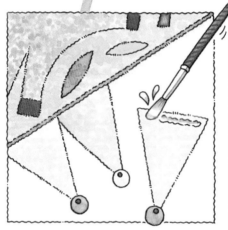

4 Use the trimmings you have to make your banner as colourful as possible. Sew or glue buttons and beads to the design, and attach a fringe to the bottom edge.

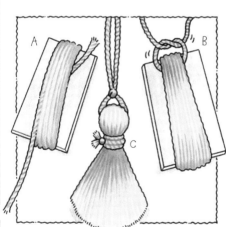

6 To make a tassel, wind yarn around a piece of card (A). Tie the yarn together at the top and remove the card (B). Wind yarn around the tassel, tie with a knot then cut through the ends (C). Attach tassels to lengths of yarn and tie to the dowels.

88

JESUS CLEARS THE TEMPLE

Jesus is angry

When Jesus arrived in Jerusalem, he set off towards the temple. He wanted to pray to God in the holy place of this noisy, bustling city.

But when Jesus entered the temple area, he saw something which made him very angry indeed. There were people buying and selling animals and doves, and other people were changing money.

The whole place had become a noisy, smelly market place, just like the rest of the city.

Jesus turned over the tables with a great crash. The doves flew away. The people behind the tables were shocked. What was Jesus doing?

You will need:

✂

Small round box
e.g. empty cheese box

Scissors
(and some adult help)

Ruler

24cm x 4cm
balsa wood strip

Poster paints
and brush

7 x 35cm
lengths of string

Large blunt needle

3 large
wooden beads

1 Ask an adult to help you make three holes an *equal distance apart* from each other in the rims of the lid and *base* of the round box, using the sharp point of the scissors.

2 Using the ruler to position them accurately, ask an adult to help you make three holes in the *balsa wood strip*, again using the point of the scissors. Make a hole exactly in the *centre* of the strip and one hole 2cm from either end.

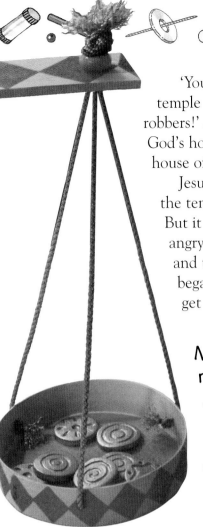

'You are turning the temple into a den of robbers!' shouted Jesus. 'It is God's house. It should be a house of prayer!'

Jesus wanted to keep the temple a holy place. But it made many people angry. The chief priests and teachers of the law began to make plans to get rid of Jesus.

Make these moneylenders' scales like the ones used in the temple courts.

3 Use the poster paints to paint the lid and base of the box and the balsa wood strip. Moneylenders' scales would have been made from metal, but you can paint your scales with bright patterns.

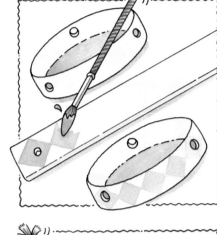

4 Thread a length of string through each of the three holes in the lid of the box and tie a knot at the end of each string. Use the large blunt needle to thread the three lengths through the hole in the end of the strip and through a bead, then tie the three ends together.

5 Repeat these instructions and attach the base of the card box to the other end of the strip in the same way. Thread the needle with the last piece of string and tie a knot in the end of the string. Thread it through a bead, then through the centre hole and tie a loop in the end.

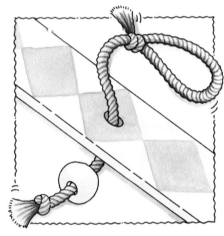

6 If you have measured and made your scales accurately, they should be evenly balanced when you hold them up by the central string. Use small coins as weights and use your scales to weigh out sweets or small pieces of fruit and nuts. (For coins, see pages 92-93.)

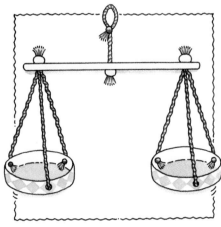

90

MARY'S GIFT TO JESUS

The smell of perfume fills the room

Shortly before Passover, Jesus went to eat at a friend's house. A woman called Mary came up to Jesus, holding a small but very precious alabaster jar.

When Mary opened the jar, the sweet smell of perfume wafted out. Mary had brought a very expensive gift for Jesus. She poured it over his head.

'What's she doing?' asked some of Jesus' friends. 'That's a real waste of money, just pouring it away like that!'

Jesus heard them complaining and said quietly, 'Leave her alone. She has shown how much she loves me. She has done a beautiful thing.'

You will need:

✂

Small glass jar with screw top lid, e.g. herb or spice jar

Paper kitchen towel

Small plastic ping-pong ball

PVA glue and brush

Poster paints and brush

Metallic poster paints

Small beads, needle and thread for decoration

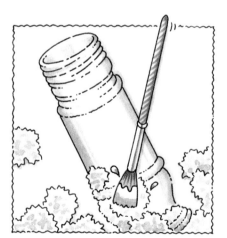

Remove the lid from the clean glass jar and brush an area of the surface with PVA glue. Tear up small pieces of kitchen towel and stick them to the surface but avoid gluing the paper to the screw top rim.

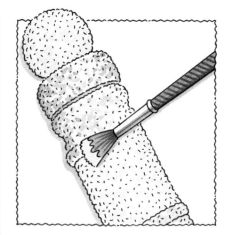

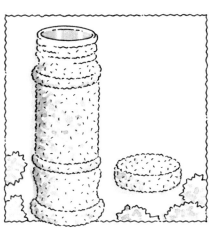

2 Continue to cover the surface of the jar, making sure that the paper remains crinkly. Cover the lid, keeping it separate from the jar. Leave to dry and then add more layers to give an extra crinkly texture to the surface.

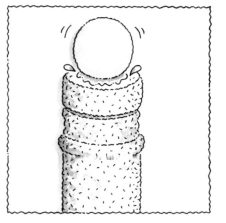

3 Glue the plastic ball to the top of the lid and cover it with the glued kitchen paper so it has a crinkly texture to match the jar.

4 When the jar and lid are completely dry, paint them both using brightly coloured poster paints. The perfume jar that Mary used was made of alabaster and would have looked very plain, but you can decorate your perfume jar to make it look very special. Leave to dry.

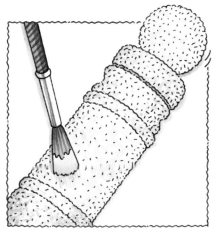

5 To make the jar look very expensive, brush a thin coat of gold or silver paint sparingly over the surface, making sure the first colour still shows through.

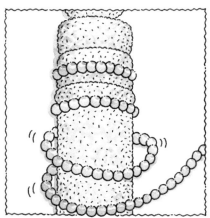

6 Finally, decorate the perfume jar. Thread very small beads on to a length of thread and tie the ends firmly. Wind the thread of beads around the jar and glue them firmly in place.

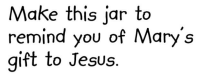

Make this jar to remind you of Mary's gift to Jesus.

92

THIRTY PIECES OF SILVER

Judas becomes a traitor

The chief priests wanted to get rid of Jesus. But they didn't know how to capture him.

Judas Iscariot, who had been one of Jesus' closest friends, was greedy for money. He thought of a plan to get rich quick.

Judas went to the chief priests and asked, 'What will you pay me if I hand Jesus over to you?'

'We'll give you thirty pieces of silver,' they said.

'Done!' said Judas.

Judas watched for a chance to hand Jesus over to them. He was no longer a friend of Jesus. He was his enemy.

You will need:

✂

TO MAKE THE COINS

Self-hardening clay

Rolling pin and wooden or plastic board

Small cocktail sticks, pencils and carving tools

Round plastic bottle top

Sheets of paper kitchen towel

Silver poster paint and brush

TO MAKE THE MONEY BAG

15cm x 30cm piece of felt

Needle, thread and scissors

40cm length of cord

Scraps of felt and beads

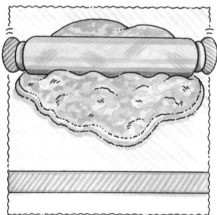

1 Using the rolling pin, roll out the clay on the board to an even thickness of about 0.5cm.

2 Use the round plastic lid as a cutter to cut out thirty circular shapes from the clay. Carefully remove these clay circles from the board and place them on the kitchen towel.

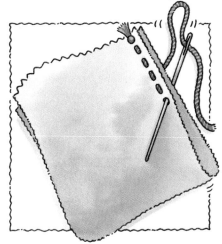

93

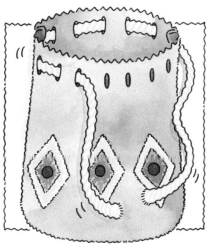

Make these silver
coins as a reminder
of how Judas turned
against Jesus.

5 Coins were often kept safe in small
money bags made from leather or
cloth. To make the bag, fold the rectangle
of felt in half and sew along two sides using
a small simple running stitch.

6 Turn the bag inside out so the stitching
is on the inside. Decorate the bag by
gluing on scraps of felt and beads. Ask an
adult to make a line of small holes about
2cm from the opening with the scissors.
Thread the cord in and out of the holes.
Thread a small bead on to each end
and secure with a knot. Fray
the ends then tie the ends
together. Keep your silver
coins in the money bag
and pull the cord
tight to keep
them safe.

3 Use the small sticks and tools to
decorate the clay circles, making them
look like coins. Roman coins were often
decorated with the head of the emperor,
but you can think of your own designs. Try
to keep the coins flat and leave the clay to
dry out completely.

4 When the clay coins are dry, use the
poster paint to paint them silver. Paint
one side and leave to dry before turning
over to paint the reverse side.

JESUS WASHES HIS FRIENDS' FEET

Jesus shows his friends how much he loves them

Jesus knew that he would not be with his friends for much longer. He wanted to celebrate the Passover meal with them one last time. It was a special time of remembering how God had rescued Moses and the Israelites from slavery in Egypt many years ago.

Jesus met his twelve friends at the upper room of a house in Jerusalem.

Jesus took a bowl of water and began to wash his friends' feet.

'You mustn't wash my feet!' said Peter. 'You are our master, not our servant!'

'Unless I wash you, you don't belong to me,' said Jesus.

'Then wash my hands and head as well!' said Peter.

Jesus washed Peter's feet.

'Now that I have washed your feet,' said Jesus, 'you must also wash each other's feet. Do as I have done.'

You will need:

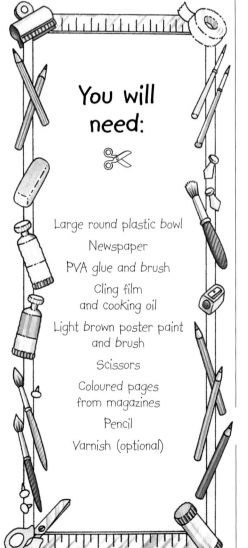

Large round plastic bowl

Newspaper

PVA glue and brush

Cling film and cooking oil

Light brown poster paint and brush

Scissors

Coloured pages from magazines

Pencil

Varnish (optional)

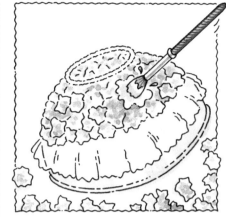

1 Use the round plastic bowl as your mould. Lightly grease the outside with the oil and cover with the cling film. Cover the outside of the bowl with six layers of newspaper pieces glued with diluted PVA. The design of this papier mâché bowl is fairly shallow so you will only need to cover about 20cm up the sides.

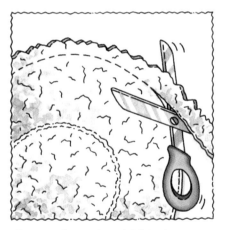

2 Leave the papier mâché to dry overnight, then remove it from the plastic bowl by pulling away the cling film. Neaten the papier mâché bowl by trimming around the edges with the scissors.

3 Neaten the edge of the bowl further by gluing small strips of glued newspaper around the rim. Leave to dry.

4 When it is dry, paint the bowl inside and out with a light brown colour to make the bowl look as if it is made from clay. Decorate the bowl with a simple mosaic pattern. Draw the outline in pencil around the rim of the bowl and include a small design in the centre.

5 Cut out lots of small squares from the coloured pages of magazines and arrange all the squares into groups of similar colours to make the mosaics. This design does not cover the bowl completely, but makes a border pattern and central design.

6 Follow the pencil guide lines and glue the coloured squares to the surface of the bowl with PVA. Build up the mosaic pattern and overlap the squares if necessary. When you have finished decorating the bowl, you could varnish it to help strengthen and protect the mosaic.

Make this mosaic bowl and think about how much Jesus loved his friends.

THE LAST SUPPER
Jesus shares a special meal

After Jesus had finished washing everyone's feet, he reclined at the table with his friends, ready to eat the Passover meal of roasted lamb, bread without yeast, bitter herbs and wine.

Jesus looked at his friends gathered around him.

You will need:

✂

2 clean plastic dessert pots

Plastic cotton reel

Scissors

String, split peas and lentils

Paper kitchen towel

Sticky tape

PVA glue and brush

Cocktail stick

Silver or brown poster paint

Paint brush

Make this special cup to remember Jesus' words at the Last Supper.

'One of you is going to hand me over to be killed,' he said.
His friends were very worried.
'Surely not I!' each one said to another.
Jesus already knew it would be Judas Iscariot.
While they were eating, Jesus took the bread, broke it and gave it to his friends.
'Eat this and remember me,' said Jesus. 'This is my body.'
Then he took the cup of wine, thanked God for it, and handed it round.
'Drink this and remember me,' said Jesus. 'This is my blood, given for many.'
Jesus' friends drank the wine. They sang a song together, then went out to the Mount of Olives.

1 Use the scissors carefully to cut out the bottom section of one of the dessert pots to form the base of the cup. Tip this upside down, as shown here. The cotton reel will form the stem of the cup.

2 Use the PVA to glue the cotton reel between the two pots and leave to dry.

3 Brush the surface with PVA glue and begin to cover the pots with torn pieces of paper towel. The layers of paper towel will help to hold the two plastic pots and the cotton reel together. Make sure the paper remains nice and crinkly. Cover the whole surface inside and out with at least two layers of paper and leave to dry.

4 Wind a length of string around the rim of the cup, fixing the string in place with dabs of glue. Then glue string around the stem and the base of the cup and leave to dry.

5 Make a raised pattern on the surface of the cup with split peas and lentils. Place small blobs of PVA glue on the surface using the cocktail stick and carefully position the peas and lentils on the glue.

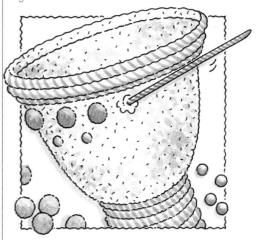

6 When you have finished decorating the cup, leave the glue to dry. Then paint the cup inside and out with the silver or brown poster paint. It is likely that the cup Jesus used would have been made of earthenware. Today the cups used in churches tend to be made of silver.

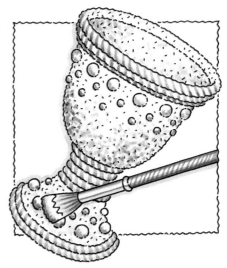

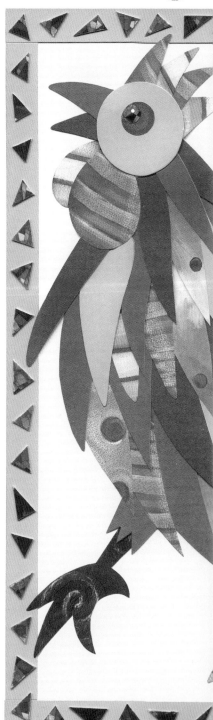

PETER LETS JESUS DOWN

Peter tells lies to save himself

Jesus' twelve friends had spent a lot of time with him.

Peter was one of his three closest friends. But Jesus knew that Peter was going to let him down.

Shortly before Jesus was arrested and taken away to be killed, he warned Peter:

'Before the cock crows tonight, you will say three times that you do not know me.'

Peter was very upset. Jesus was his friend!

But then Jesus was taken away by soldiers.

Peter was waiting to see what would happen, when some girls came up to him and asked if he was a friend of Jesus.

'No,' said Peter, 'I don't know what you are talking about!'

They asked him three times and each time he said, 'No!'

Then suddenly a cock crowed. Peter remembered what Jesus had said.

Peter felt terrible and cried bitterly.

He had wanted to be a good friend to Jesus, but now he had let Jesus down.

You will need:

✂

Sheet of thin coloured card

Glue stick

Sheets of coloured paper

Pencil

Scraps of coloured wrapping papers

Scissors

1 Sketch out a simple outline of a cockerel on the sheet of coloured card. Draw in the main details and features. Draw a border design around the edge.

2 Draw lots of different sized feathers on the sheets of coloured paper. Follow the shapes on your design and draw the claw and leg shapes and large tail feathers. Cut out the shapes carefully.

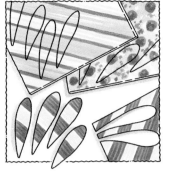

Make this collage of a crowing cockerel.

3 Cut out shapes to make the border pattern and glue them around the edge, following your outline.

4 Use the glue stick to glue the feather shapes on to your sketch. Start with the tail feathers and overlap them, using a selection of different colours. Then glue down the claw and leg shapes.

5 The body feathers will hide the ends of the tail feathers and the legs. Start at the bottom of the cockerel and glue the feathers down. Follow the body shape of the cockerel and overlap the feathers as you work up to the neck. Make sure all the background card is covered up in between the feathers.

6 Cut out shapes for the beak and the head feathers and glue them in place. Cut out a circle for the head and glue that over the top. Then add the eye.

JESUS DIES
Jesus is nailed to a cross

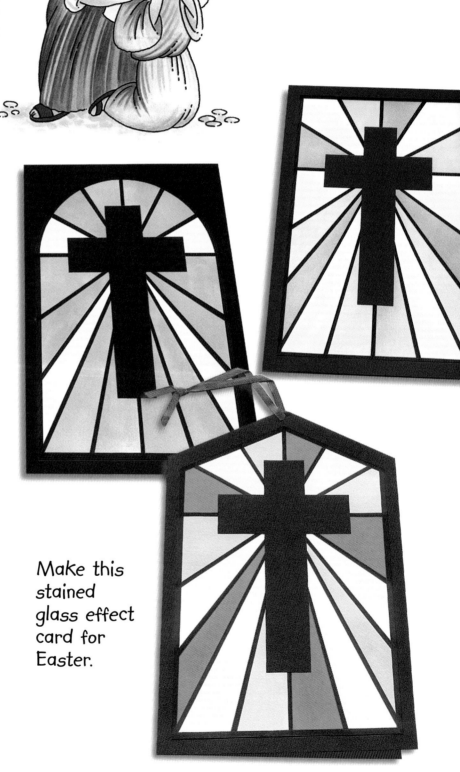

You will need:

✂

Sheets of A4 dark
coloured card

Sheets of
A4 white paper

Glue stick

Poster paints and brush,
or
coloured felt tipped pens

Thick black felt tipped pen

Scissors

Pencil

Ruler

Make this
stained
glass effect
card for
Easter.

 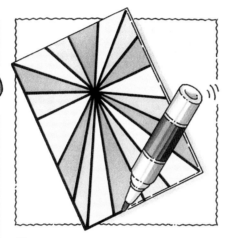 

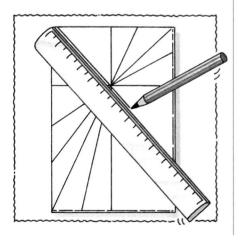  

Jesus only ever did good things and helped other people, but he had many enemies. They wanted him out of the way. Jesus wanted to show people God's love, but they didn't always want to listen.

After Jesus was arrested and tried, he was taken away by soldiers and nailed to a cross. It was a terrible day. Jesus' mother, Mary, stood close by and watched. How could they do this to her precious son? John, another of Jesus' friends, stood by and comforted her. Many of the women who had followed Jesus stood and wept.

Jesus died. His body was taken down from the cross and placed in a tomb.

Jesus' friends thought they would never see him again.

101

1 Cut a sheet of A4 white paper in half and trim a 1cm strip from all the four sides to make sure the design will fit on the finished card.

3 Colour in the rays with poster paints or felt tipped pens. Then draw over the original pencil lines with the thick black felt tipped pen. Also draw a black line around the edge of the design.

5 Use the ruler and pencil to draw a simple cross shape on the dark card and cut it out. Then glue the cross on to the centre of the design so that the coloured rays shine out from behind the cross.

2 Make a central point on the white paper, roughly 6cm from the top. Then use the ruler to draw lines radiating out from this point to the edges of the paper.

4 Fold a sheet of coloured card in half. Carefully glue the design to the front of the folded card using the glue stick.

6 Use the method to make more cards. Try making different shaped cards, as shown here, with different colour schemes. To make the window hanging, you will need only half the A4 sheet of coloured card, but make two cross designs and glue one on each side.

JESUS IS ALIVE!
The empty tomb

It was three days since Jesus had died on the cross. All his friends were heartbroken and didn't know what to do next. Some of the women went to his tomb early on Sunday morning, but they had a shock! The large stone which blocked the entrance to the tomb had been rolled away!

Inside the tomb, Jesus' body had gone. All that was left were strips of cloth which the body had been wrapped in. Suddenly two men in bright shining clothes appeared.

'Don't look for Jesus here,' they said. 'He's alive!'

The women couldn't believe it! They ran home at once and told Jesus' friends.

Very soon they saw Jesus again for themselves. It was true! Jesus was alive!

You will need:

✂

Large round lid (a lid from a large biscuit tin is ideal)

Black, brown and white poster paint and brush

Collection of small pieces of dried bark and twigs

Collection of small fresh flowers, leaves and moss

Collection of different sized stones and pebbles*

Gravel*

PVA glue and brush

Paper Kitchen towel

* Health and safety precaution: these materials should be washed thoroughly before children handle them.

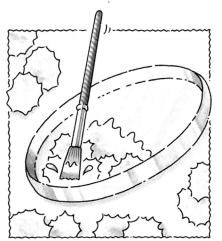

1 First you will need to disguise the shiny tin lid. Tear up small pieces of paper towel and glue them to the inside and rim of the lid with PVA, giving the surface a rough texture.

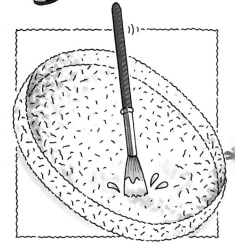

2 Make sure the shiny surface is completely covered, especially around the outside of the rim, then leave to dry. Paint the textured surface with brown and white paint, giving it a dappled finish.

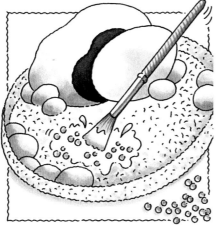

3 The largest pebble will represent the tomb. Use the black paint to paint a circular shape on the side of the pebble to represent the entrance to the tomb.

4 Position the large pebble on the lid and find another pebble to represent the stone that would have been rolled in front of the entrance hole. Glue these in place with PVA.

5 Arrange the rest of the smaller stones around the edge of the lid and next to the large pebbles and glue these in place. Then brush the inside of the lid with PVA and sprinkle gravel into the glue.

Make this miniature garden scene to show Jesus' empty tomb.

6 Place the small pieces of dried bark, twigs, small flowers, leaves and moss in your Easter garden.

BREAKFAST ON THE BEACH

Jesus eats with his disciples

Over the next few days, Jesus appeared to his friends, showing them that he really was alive again.

One night, Peter and a group of disciples were out fishing in their boat. They had caught nothing. Early the next morning, Jesus stood on the shore, watching them. He was far away, so they couldn't see at first who it was.

'Haven't you caught any fish?' he shouted to the fishermen.

'No!' said Peter.

'Then throw your net on the other side of the boat,' said Jesus, 'and you will catch plenty!'

The men did as he said and sure enough, their nets were filled to bursting point with fresh, wriggling fish.

'It's Jesus!' said Peter. They knew that only Jesus could do something so amazing. Peter was so excited that he jumped out of the boat and swam to shore.

Jesus had made a small fire ready on the shore to cook some of the fish. He had some bread for them too. His friends came and sat with him and ate breakfast on the beach. It was wonderful to be with Jesus again!

You will need:

35cm x 50cm piece of pale blue felt

Black felt tipped pen

Selection of scraps of coloured felt, fabric and netting

PVA glue and brush

White card and pencil

Scissors

Buttons, beads and trimmings for decoration

Cocktail sticks

60cm length of wooden dowel

2 plasticine balls

Draw one large and one small simple fish shape on the card. Cut the card shapes out carefully.

Make this wall hanging of the symbol of the fish, used by those who believe in Jesus.

5 Cut out two strips of fabric to fit along the two sides of the hanging and glue these in place. Then glue the small fish on top of these strips to make the border patterns. If you have any small buttons or beads, use them to decorate the fish.

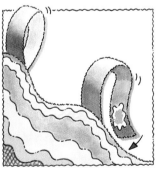

6 Cut out four strips of fabric to make loops along the top edge of the hanging and glue in place. Thread the wooden dowel through the loops and push a plasticine ball on each end to hold the hanging in place.

2 Lay the card template on the fabric, draw around the shape with the felt tipped pen and cut it out. You will need two large fish and eight small ones. If you have a selection of fabrics, cut them out using different colours and patterns.

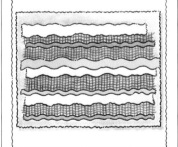

3 Cut out a number of wavy strips of coloured fabric and glue them across the background felt to make an underwater scene. Use blue, grey and green coloured netting and wavy trimmings. Don't worry about lining up the ends of the wavy strips along the two sides as these will be covered by the border pattern.

4 Glue the two large fish on to the centre of the scene, over the top of the waves. Cut out a number of fabric circles and glue these to the bodies of the fish to represent their scales.

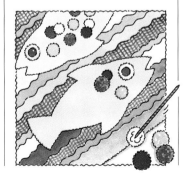

106

PENTECOST
The Holy Spirit comes in power

Make this Pentecost prayer book to give as a gift or use yourself.

You will need:

✂

Small notebook

Ruler

Piece of plain, brightly coloured paper

Selection of coloured holographic papers and foil in yellows, golds, and fiery colours

Scissors

Glue stick

Small strips of card for the bookmarks

At the festival of Pentecost, the disciples were gathered together. It was some time since Jesus had returned to his Father God in heaven. But Jesus had promised to send his helper, the Holy Spirit, to them.

Suddenly there was sound like the rushing of a mighty wind. Tongues of fire came to rest on each of them.

The disciples, full of the Holy Spirit, then spoke in many different languages

1 Take the notebook and measure the width and the length of the front cover. Subtract 1cm from both measurements to give you the size of the front panel design.

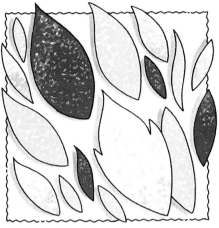

3 Draw different sizes of 'tongues of fire' shapes on the coloured foils and holographic papers. Cut out the largest shapes first.

5 Finally, cut out the very smallest flame shapes and glue them in place. Use the coloured foils and holographic papers if you have them, as they will make the tongues of fire sparkle and glow.

2 Cut a piece of plain, brightly coloured paper to the size of the front panel measurements to be the background to the flame design. Stick the paper to the front of the notebook using the glue stick.

4 Glue the large shapes to the cover first and build up the design, gluing further smaller shapes on top. Use contrasting colours and textures and place different papers on top of each other.

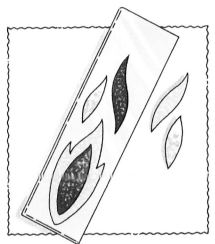

6 Use the small strip of thin, coloured card to make the bookmark and decorate it with the flame shapes to match the notebook cover.

and visitors to Jerusalem from different countries each understood what was being said in their own language. Peter began to tell the crowds about Jesus and how he forgave all who said sorry to God for the bad things they had done.

People were amazed! Many came to follow Jesus. The new believers were known as Christians. They shared their food and belongings with one another, and cared for others as Jesus had taught them.

Where to find the stories in the Bible

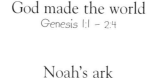

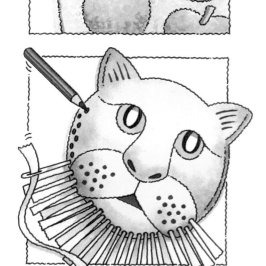

God made the world
Genesis 1:1 – 2:4

Noah's ark
Genesis 6:12 – 8:22

The tower of Babel
Genesis 11:1-9

God's promise to Abraham
Genesis 15:1-6; 21:1-7

Rebekah's kindness
Genesis 24:10-67

Jacob and Esau
Genesis 25:24-34

Joseph's coat
Genesis 37:1-4

Joseph's dreams
Genesis 37:1-11

Joseph interprets dreams
Genesis 39:6-40:23

Moses in the bulrushes
Exodus 1:6-16; 2:1-10

The golden lampstand
Exodus 25:31-40

Gideon's victory
Judges 7:15-25

The strength of Samson
Judges 14:5-6; 16:4-30

David's harp
1 Samuel 16:14-23

David and Goliath
1 Samuel 17:4-50

Daniel in the lions' den
Daniel 6

Jonah and the big fish
Jonah 1 – 3

An angel visits Mary
Luke 1:26-38, 46-55

Mary and Joseph
travel to Bethlehem
Luke 2:1-5

Bethlehem is full
Luke 2:1-7

Jesus is born
Luke 2:6-7

The shepherds' surprise
Luke 2:8-14

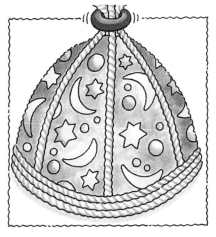

Look out for other titles in this series:
Christmas Make & Do
Easter Make & Do
Celebrations Make & Do

GILLIAN CHAPMAN
Christmas Make & Do
Craft ideas inspired by the story
of the first Christmas

Gillian Chapman
Easter Make & Do
Craft ideas which bring
the story of Easter to life

Gillian Chapman
Celebrations Make & Do
Craft ideas which bring
the festivals to life

All available from Barnabas: visit www.barnabasforchildren.org.uk.